# Explore
## the Bible.

**Let the Word dwell in you.**

P9-CAN-231

*EXPLORE THE BIBLE: Esther*

© 2014 LifeWay Press® • Reprinted December 2017

ISBN 978-1-4300-4012-5 • Item 005725122

Dewey decimal classification: 222.9
Subject headings: BIBLE. O.T. ESTHER \
WOMEN \ COURAGE

**ERIC GEIGER**
*Vice President, LifeWay Resources*

**MICHAEL KELLEY**
*Director, Groups Ministry*

**TONY EVANS**
*General Editor*

**JEREMY MAXFIELD**
*Content Editor*

Send questions/comments to: Content Editor, *Explore the Bible: Adult Small-Group Study;* One LifeWay Plaza; Nashville, TN 37234.

*Printed in the United States of America*

For ordering or inquiries visit LifeWay.com; write to LifeWay Small Groups; One LifeWay Plaza; Nashville, TN 37234; or call toll free 800-458-2772.

With *Explore the Bible* groups can expect to engage Scripture in its proper context and be better prepared to live it out in their own context. These book-by-book studies will help participants—

> grow in their love for Scripture;

> gain new knowledge about what the Bible teaches;

> develop biblical disciplines;

> internalize the Word in a way that transforms their lives.

Session 1 quotation: Tony Evans, *For Married Women Only* (Chicago: Moody, 2010), 28. Session 2 quotation: Tony Evans, *Kingdom Man* (Nashville: Thomas Nelson, 2012), 19. Session 3 quotation: William Shakespeare, *Macbeth*, in *Shakespeare: Major Plays and the Sonnets*, ed. G. B. Harrison (New York: Harcourt, Brace & World, 1948), 4.3.209–10. References are to act, scene, and lines. Session 4 quotation: Michael Card, *The Walk* (Nashville: Thomas Nelson, 2001). Session 5 quotation: Tony Evans, *Our God Is Awesome* (Chicago: Moody, 1994), 163. Session 6 quotation: Tony Evans, *Raising Kingdom Kids* (Carol Stream, IL: Tyndale, 2014), 27.

### Connect

 @ExploreTheBible

 facebook.com/explorethebible

 lifeway.com/explorethebible

 ministrygrid.com/web/explorethebible

# >ABOUT THIS STUDY

**THE INVISIBLE HAND OF GOD IS AT WORK IN AND THROUGH YOU.**

What if everything in your seemingly ordinary life is leading toward an extraordinary display of God's greatness? You're not where you are by accident. There's no such thing as luck or coincidence. God has a plan, and you're right in the middle of the action.

Will your heart break and compel you to boldly take a stand and speak for those without a voice? Will you live with conviction but respect? Will God bring salvation to people within your circle of influence?

The Book of Esther gives hope and confidence to anyone who needs to know that God is present, powerful, and personal. He has strategically positioned you as part of His kingdom to bring salvation to your circle of influence.

***Explore the Bible: Esther*** helps you know and apply the encouraging and empowering truth of God's Word. Each session is organized in the following way.

UNDERSTAND THE CONTEXT: This page explains the original context of each passage and begins relating the primary themes to your life today.

EXPLORE THE TEXT: These pages walk you through Scripture, providing helpful commentary and encouraging thoughtful interaction with God through His Word.

OBEY THE TEXT: This page helps you apply the truths you've explored. It's not enough to know what the Bible says. God's Word has the power to change your life.

LEADER GUIDE: This final section provides optional discussion starters and suggested questions to help anyone lead a group in reviewing each section of the personal study.

For helps on how to use *Explore The Bible*, tips on how to better lead groups, or additional ideas for leading, visit: **www.ministrygrid.com/web/ExploreTheBible.**

# ❯ GROUP COMMITMENT

As you begin this study, it's important that everyone agrees to key group values. Clearly establishing the purpose of your time together will foster healthy expectations and help ease any uncertainties. The goal is to ensure that everyone has a positive experience leading to spiritual growth and true community. Initial each value as you discuss the following with your group.

❏ PRIORITY

Life is busy, but we value this time with one another and with God's Word. We choose to make being together a priority.

❏ PARTICIPATION

We're a group. Everyone is encouraged to participate. No one dominates.

❏ RESPECT

Everyone is given the right to his or her own opinions. All questions are encouraged and respected.

❏ TRUST

Each person humbly seeks truth through time in prayer and in the Bible. We trust God as the loving authority in our lives.

❏ CONFIDENTIALITY

Anything said in our meetings is never repeated outside the group without the permission of everyone involved. This commitment is vital in creating an environment of trust and openness.

❏ SUPPORT

Everyone can count on anyone in this group. Permission is given to call on one another at any time, especially in times of crisis. The group provides care for every member.

❏ ACCOUNTABILITY

We agree to let the members of our group hold us accountable to commitments we make in the loving ways we decide on. Questions are always welcome. Unsolicited advice, however, isn't permitted.

_____          _____

I agree to all the commitments.                              Date

# ❯ GENERAL EDITOR

 **Dr. Tony Evans** is one of America's most respected leaders in evangelical circles. He is a pastor, a best-selling author, and a frequent speaker at Bible conferences and seminars throughout the nation.

Dr. Evans has served as the senior pastor of Oak Cliff Bible Fellowship in Dallas, Texas, for more than 35 years. He is also the founder and president of The Urban Alternative, a ministry that seeks to restore hope and transform lives through the proclamation and application of God's Word.

Dr. Evans is the author of more than 50 books, including the following LifeWay short-term Bible studies: *Victory in Spiritual Warfare, Kingdom Man, Kingdom Agenda, It's Not Too Late, Horizontal Jesus,* and *The Power of God's Names.* For information about these Bible studies, please visit *lifeway.com/tonyevans.*

# ❯ CONTENTS

# BEAUTY, HONOR, AND INFLUENCE

The invisible hand of God is at work in the lives
of both those who know Him and those who don't.

# ❯ ABOUT THE BOOK OF ESTHER

The Bible is filled with accounts of men and women who trusted in God and took courageous stands to live for Him. Although some of them faced the fearful prospect of martyrdom, they didn't back down from their devotion to the living God. God used these men and women—individuals like Esther—to advance His kingdom purposes.

The Book of Esther is one of the more controversial books of the Old Testament. How can we have a book in the Bible that never mentions God's name in any form or fashion? This is the only book in the Bible without an explicit mention of God or even a mention of the law and worship. Yet, though never explicit, the invisible hand of God is undeniable and implicit throughout every detail of the story.

## AUTHOR

The Book of Esther doesn't name its writer. Early Jewish and Christian traditions suggest that among the people named in the book, Mordecai, Esther's cousin and guardian, was in the best position to record the events. Scripture says Mordecai recorded certain events in order to relate them to Jews throughout the kingdom (see Esth. 9:20). The writer possessed great literary skill, especially in developing plot and narrative tension.

## DATE

In terms of the events covered in the book, the narrative of Esther covers 486 to 465 B.C., during the years of Ahasuerus's reign over Persia. In terms of when the books were written, we can't be certain. If written by Mordecai, the Book of Esther was probably written soon after the events described. Like Ezra and Nehemiah, the book is set in the fifth century B.C. as the long decades of the Babylonian exile were drawing to a close. Challenges and dangers still abounded for God's people. Yet God called out bold individuals who were born "for such a time as this" (Esth. 4:14).

## PURPOSE

The Book of Esther concludes with a clear purpose: for the original audience to understand and observe the celebration of Purim. The events of Esther's life unfolded in a way that revealed God's providential care for His people. Because of the boldness and selfless faith of an unlikely heroine, God's people were freed to defend themselves against and ultimately be delivered from evil.

God wouldn't allow His plan of salvation to fail. Whether behind the scenes (providence) or by direct answer to His people's prayers, God ensured the success of His purposes. His activity in the Book of Esther included preserving the people through whom He would send the Messiah, Jesus Christ, to provide salvation from sin to all who believe in Him.

## Think About It

*The story of Esther is driven by conversations leading to actions.*

*Circle words related to speech.*

*Underline words describing reactions.*

**1:10** On the seventh day, when the king was feeling good from the wine, Ahasuerus commanded Mehuman, Biztha, Harbona, Bigtha, Abagtha, Zethar, and Carkas, the seven eunuchs who personally served him, **11** to bring Queen Vashti before him with her royal crown. He wanted to show off her beauty to the people and the officials, because she was very beautiful. **12** But Queen Vashti refused to come at the king's command that was delivered by his eunuchs. The king became furious and his anger burned within him. **15** The king asked, "According to the law, what should be done with Queen Vashti, since she refused to obey King Ahasuerus's command that was delivered by the eunuchs?"

**2:2** The king's personal attendants suggested, "Let a search be made for beautiful young women for the king. **4** Then the young woman who pleases the king will become queen instead of Vashti." This suggestion pleased the king, and he did accordingly. **5** In the fortress of Susa, there was a Jewish man named Mordecaia son of Jair, son of Shimei, son of Kish, a Benjaminite. **6** He had been taken into exile from Jerusalem with the other captives when King Nebuchadnezzar of Babylon took King Jeconiaha of Judah into exile. **7** Mordecai was the legal guardian of his cousin Hadassah (that is, Esther), because she didn't have a father or mother. The young woman had a beautiful figure and was extremely good-looking. When her father and mother died, Mordecai had adopted her as his own daughter. **8** When the king's command and edict became public knowledge, many young women gathered at the fortress of Susa under Hegai's care. Esther was also taken to the palace and placed under the care of Hegai, who was in charge of the women. **9** The young woman pleased him and gained his favor so that he accelerated the process of the beauty treatments and the special diet that she received. He assigned seven hand-picked female servants to her from the palace and transferred her and her servants to the harem's best quarters. **10** Esther did not reveal her ethnic background or her birthplace, because Mordecai had ordered her not to. **11** Every day Mordecai took a walk in front of the harem's courtyard to learn how Esther was doing and to see what was happening to her. **17** The king loved Esther more than all the other women. She won more favor and approval from him than did any of the other young women. He placed the royal crown on her head and made her queen in place of Vashti. **20** Esther still had not revealed her birthplace or her ethnic background, as Mordecai had directed. She obeyed Mordecai's orders, as she always had while he raised her.

# ❯ UNDERSTAND THE CONTEXT

USE THE FOLLOWING PAGES TO PREPARE FOR YOUR GROUP TIME.

This biblical account of intrigue and "fate" is set in ancient Persia—formerly Mesopotamia, the region around modern-day Iraq and Iran. The king who became Esther's husband, Ahasuerus (Xerxes), reigned in Persia from 486 to 465 B.C. after the death of his father, Darius.

God's covenant people, the Jews, had previously been captured by the Babylonians and were living as exiles under a pagan king, Nebuchadnezzar (see Dan. 1–2). When the Persians overthrew the Babylonians in 539 B.C., as Daniel's interpretation of Nebuchadnezzar's dream prophesied, Jews were granted freedom from their Babylonian exile. Cyrus's edict in 538 B.C. allowed many Jews to return to rebuild Jerusalem (see Ezra 1:1-5). Many others remained in their deported regions and assimilated into Persian society, much as immigrants today assimilate into the "melting pot" that is American society.

Persian kings were concerned to perpetuate unity and compliance within the realm, which would sustain both the empire's endurance and defense against a foreign power. The cunning of the Persian rulers in instituting empire-wide policies and social structures to unify its people and culture surely contributed to the empire's vast geography and endurance. In addition to tiered governance, a few other cultural developments included embracing the diversity of cultures present among such a vast populace; the policy of emancipating slaves, including the Jewish people (see Ezra 1:1-5); instituting postal and road systems; and importantly, promoting an official language throughout the land—Aramaic (the language in which some of the divinely inspired Old Testament is written as a result). All these developments play a role in revealing the invisible God through the story of Esther.

"A GODLY WOMAN'S TRUE ADORNMENT CAN'T BE BOUGHT AT A DEPARTMENT STORE OR ACQUIRED IN THE BEAUTY SHOP."
—*Dr. Tony Evans*

1. The Persian Empire extended from India to Cush (see Esth. 1:1). Mesopotamia was the land between the Euphrates and Tigris Rivers and was included under early Persian dominion as the Achaemenid Empire, founded in the 6th century B.C. by Cyrus the Great. The events of Esther took place in the capital city of Susa, the winter capital and one of three capital cities. Ecbatana and Persepolis were the other two. Some assert that Babylon was also a capital city.

# ❯ EXPLORE THE TEXT

## *PERSIA NEEDED A NEW QUEEN* (Esther 1:10-12,15)

Our story opens with the great pomp and circumstance that was common among the Persians as King Ahasuerus declared a 180-day festival to celebrate his splendor and the splendor of the Medo-Persian Empire. The king concluded this half-year festival with a week-long party for all the people in the capital fortress city of Susa, where he would further exhibit his splendor, including the beauty of his wife, Queen Vashti.

The king was perhaps uninhibited because he "was feeling good from the wine" (v. 10). Such a picture of an intoxicated king would probably conjure in the minds of the original Jewish readers a previous drunken ruler. Belshazzar was the king of the Babylonian Empire when, also in a drunken stupor and wanting to display the splendor of his dominion, he literally saw the writing on the wall that God was about to bring his kingdom to an end and give it to the Medes and the Persians (see Dan. 5:5,25-28).

When Vashti refused to be put on display, "the king became furious and his anger burned within him" (Esth. 1:12). Ahasuerus promptly recognized that his authority was being challenged before the entire kingdom. The most powerful man on the planet and the commander of an army at war with Greece couldn't afford to have his authority publicly rejected.

What was to be done to one of the king's subjects who disobeyed the command of the king, even his own wife? Ahasuerus summoned his counselors and experts in the very specific and irrevocable "laws of Persia and Media" (v. 19; also see 8:8; Dan. 6:8,12) to determine what should be done with Vashti, "according to the law" (Esth. 1:15). Interestingly, rather than referring to a specific Medo-Persian law, "the law" in this case seems to have been what the king and his counselors wanted it to be. The determination was that Vashti was to be replaced by one "more worthy than she" (v. 19).

*In what ways might God use pride in the hearts of individuals to redirect circumstances for greater purposes?*

## GOD PROVIDED A NEW QUEEN
### *(Esther 2:2,4-8,17,20)*

Who would be the new Queen of Persia? By the authority of the king and his personal attendants, the empire-wide Miss Persia Beauty Pageant would determine the new queen. What better circumstance could avail themselves for God to raise up the beautiful, godly woman of His own choosing and for His own purposes from among millions of Persian citizens? Enter the young and "extremely good-looking" (v. 7) cousin of Mordecai, Esther.

Esther's beauty was enhanced by her respectful, humble, and submissive demeanor. She was a young woman of character who "won approval in the sight of everyone who saw her" (v. 15) and "won more favor and approval from [the king] than did any of the other young women," so much that the king "placed the royal crown on her head and made her queen in place of Vashti" (v. 17). Moreover, Esther "obeyed Mordecai's orders, as she always had while he raised her" (v. 20). The beauty of Esther's faithful obedience was a model not only for the women of fifth-century B.C. Persia but also for all women—and men—everywhere and in all times.

*List different forms and virtues of beauty (see Ps. 149:4; 1 Pet. 3:1-6).*

Was it mere coincidence that Mordecai was a public servant "at the King's Gate" (Esth. 2:19) at this time? Was it mere coincidence that "Mordecai had adopted [Esther] as his own daughter" (v. 7)? Was it mere coincidence that Mordecai and Esther had been deported from Jerusalem to Susa under Babylonian control and were residing in Susa when Ahasuerus became king and Vashti spurned him there? Was it mere coincidence that Esther was "extremely good-looking" (v. 7)? We begin to see very quickly that not even a master chess player or a brilliant mathematician could design or anticipate so many variables to determine his desired outcome. But a sovereign God can.

Proverbs 21:1 notes:

> *A king's heart is like streams of water in the LORD's hand:*
>
> *He directs it wherever He chooses.*

Psalm 75:6-7 says:

> *Exaltation does not come from the east, the west,*
>
> *or the desert, for God is the Judge:*
>
> *He brings down one and exalts another.*

God places people in positions of power for His sovereign purposes (see Rom. 9:17). The Book of Esther clearly illustrates that the geopolitical circumstances of the world, as well as the emotional and psychological dispositions of the king and queen of the world's preeminent nation, were ordained and used by God for His purposes to redeem and preserve His covenant people.

In the New Testament the apostle John tells us:

> *No one has ever seen God.*
>
> *The One and Only Son—*
>
> *the One who is at the Father's side—*
>
> *He has revealed Him.* **John 1:18**

That is, Jesus Christ has finally and fully revealed to us the invisible God. We might legitimately ask, then, does the Old Testament reveal God to us too, and if so, how?

The Old Testament reveals the invisible God in at least two ways.

1. Because God is both infinitely wise and all-powerful, He's able to order circumstances in history so that they carry out His good purposes. Those events and circumstances put on display for all to see the many facets of God's nature—His power, His care, His wisdom, His holiness, His love, and others. Without an explanation of the purpose and meaning of those events, however, people might ascribe any number of personal or subjective meanings to them.

2. God's inspired explanation of those events—that is, Scripture— is needed to reveal Himself, His purposes in history, and His instruction to all who bear His image. Both the events and the explanation of those events reveal God to us.

Both of these realities testifying to the invisible God are clearly seen in the Book of Esther, even as the story begins in these opening chapters.

*What in your own life may have seemed lucky or coincidental at the time, but in hindsight you can see that God was at work to put you in a particular place or relationship or to grow your character?*

**BIBLE SKILL**
**Identify ways contemporaries use a word or phrase.**

An unspoken theme of the Book of Esther is the providential acts of God. Today the phrase "acts of God" is used in legal documents and common culture.

*What does the phrase "acts of God" mean today?*

*How is this usage similar to the biblical idea of providential acts of God?*

*How is today's usage of the term different?*

# ❯ OBEY THE TEXT

In a world that often seems out of control—overindulging desires, abusing power, obsessing over image, and driven by popular opinion—God's people can have great peace and hope knowing that God is still in control. If He can take an orphaned girl from a religious and ethnic minority group, recently freed from captivity as an exile in a foreign enemy nation, and make her the beloved new queen of the most powerful—and pagan—kingdom on earth, then we have nothing to worry about.

*How does your culture seem self-obsessed, godless, or generally out of control?*

*How can this group be like family to you, encouraging you to live with humility and respect, even toward people who may not share your values or beliefs?*

*Whom can you encourage? What specifically does that person need?*

*What will you do to live in a way that's contrary yet attractive to the culture around you?*

## MEMORIZE

"A king's heart is like streams of water in the LORD's hand: He directs it wherever He chooses."
Proverbs 21:1

Use the space provided to make observations and record prayer requests during the group experience for this session.

## MY THOUGHTS

Record insights and questions from the group experience.

_____
_____
_____
_____
_____
_____

## MY RESPONSE

Note specific ways you will put into practice the truth explored this week.

_____
_____
_____
_____
_____
_____

## MY PRAYERS

List specific prayer needs and answers to remember this week.

_____
_____
_____
_____
_____
_____

# CONFLICT AND INTEGRITY

Doing the right thing won't always receive an immediate reward and may even put God's people at odds with the world.

# › UNDERSTAND THE CONTEXT

USE THE FOLLOWING PAGES TO PREPARE FOR YOUR GROUP TIME.

The dictionary defines *genocide* as the deliberate and systematic destruction of a racial, ethnic, religious, or national group. Though none of us likely have personal experience of such evil, the world has suffered horrific genocides that killed millions of people.

What if Christians where you live became a target for persecution or even elimination? How would you act? How would you pray? What would you say to your family and friends?

The Book of Esther tells the story of one such threat and the way God protected His people. Though God isn't mentioned by name in the Book of Esther, He was there working behind the scenes, watching over His covenant people. God's plan of salvation was at stake, because Jesus would eventually come to the world through the Jews (see John 4:22; Rom. 1:16).

The Medo-Persian Empire was the undisputed world power. King Ahasuerus ruled an empire of 127 provinces stretching from India to Cush (see Esth. 1:1), that is, from the Indus River in modern-day Pakistan to Northern Sudan in Africa. An official governed each province who reported to the king (see Dan. 6.1-9). At its height the empire purportedly ruled about 44 percent of the world's population—a higher percentage than any world empire before or since.

Amid this vast empire's aristocracy, King Ahasuerus promoted one of his counselors to "a higher position than all the other officials" (Esth. 3:1) and commanded the entire royal staff at the King's Gate to bow down and pay homage to this official. When one of the elders refused to bow down, the conflict at the heart of the Book of Esther began.

"WHEN YOU STEP OUT YOUR DOOR EACH DAY, DO HEAVEN, EARTH, AND HELL TAKE NOTICE?"
—*Dr. Tony Evans*

**2:21** During those days while Mordecai was sitting at the King's Gate, Bigthan and Teresh, two eunuchs who guarded the king's entrance, became infuriated and planned to assassinate King Ahasuerus. **22** When Mordecai learned of the plot, he reported it to Queen Esther, and she told the king on Mordecai's behalf. **23** When the report was investigated and verified, both men were hanged on the gallows. This event was recorded in the Historical Record in the king's presence.

**3:1** After all this took place, King Ahasuerus honored Haman, son of Hammedatha the Agagite. He promoted him in rank and gave him a higher position than all the other officials. **2** The entire royal staff at the King's Gate bowed down and paid homage to Haman, because the king had commanded this to be done for him. But Mordecai would not bow down or pay homage. **3** The members of the royal staff at the King's Gate asked Mordecai, "Why are you disobeying the king's command?" **4** When they had warned him day after day and he still would not listen to them, they told Haman to see if Mordecai's actions would be tolerated, since he had told them he was a Jew. **5** When Haman saw that Mordecai was not bowing down or paying him homage, he was filled with rage. **6** And when he learned of Mordecai's ethnic identity, Haman decided not to do away with Mordecai alone. He planned to destroy all of Mordecai's people, the Jews, throughout Ahasuerus's kingdom. **7** In the first month, the month of Nisan, in King Ahasuerus's twelfth year, Pur (that is, the lot) was cast before Haman for each day in each month, and it fell on the twelfth month, the month Adar. **8** Then Haman informed King Ahasuerus, "There is one ethnic group, scattered throughout the peoples in every province of your kingdom, yet living in isolation. Their laws are different from everyone else's and they do not obey the king's laws. It is not in the king's best interest to tolerate them. **9** If the king approves, let an order be drawn up authorizing their destruction, and I will pay 375 tons of silver to the accountants for deposit in the royal treasury." **10** The king removed his signet ring from his finger and gave it to Haman son of Hammedatha the Agagite, the enemy of the Jewish people. **11** Then the king told Haman, "The money and people are given to you to do with as you see fit."

**15** The couriers left, spurred on by royal command, and the law was issued in the fortress of Susa. The king and Haman sat down to drink, while the city of Susa was in confusion.

# ❯ EXPLORE THE TEXT

## HAMAN, THE HONORED (Esther 2:21–3:6)

In the last few verses of Esther 2, a seemingly random story is inserted. It will later become clear that this detail is anything but insignificant and, rather, is part of God's providential care for His people. In its immediate context it serves as yet another example of Mordecai's selfless integrity. Overhearing a conversation between disgruntled guards, the faithful Jew spoils an assassination plot and saves the life of the pagan king. The story simply notes that the honorable deed was recorded by the king's historian, and no further details are given about any immediate reward or recognition.

*When has something you've done seemingly gone unrewarded?*

The account of Mordecai's humbly spoiling a murderous intent serves as a transition and contrast to a new character—a proud enemy with murder in his heart. Every good story has an antagonist. Haman, son of Hammedatha the Agagite, serves this role well in the story of Esther.

"After all this took place" (3:1)—that is, about four years after the empire-wide beauty pageant seated Esther on the queen's throne—Haman managed to climb the political ladder and be appointed as chief among all the king's officials. On top of that honor, the king commanded all his other court officials to bow down in Haman's presence. Mordecai, also a member of the king's court (see 2:19,21; 3:2-3), whether motivated by his commitment to the Second of the Ten Commandments (not to bow down in worship or homage to anything but God; see Ex. 20:4-5; Dan. 3:8-18) or by the long-standing Jewish-Amalekite enmity (see session 1, "Understand the Context"), refused to bow to Haman.

*In what ways do you draw the line between obedience to authority and refusal to compromise your faith in God?*

Needless to say, Haman wasn't pleased when he learned about Mordecai's refusal to bow to him and his Jewish ethnicity (see Esth. 3:5-6). Haman wouldn't tolerate this open rebellion against the law of the land—or against his pride—particularly from an enemy in a historic cultural feud. Haman determined to put an end to this centuries-long feud once and for all. His pride prompted him to assume that his high government position now enabled him to do just that. Rather than punishing only Mordecai, Haman concocted a plan to destroy every Jew throughout the Persian Empire.

The geopolitical and cultural circumstances of the world would appear to have converged perfectly to provide this opportunity for the genocide of the Jewish people. These kinds of world circumstances often appear to be under the control of emperors, führers, parliaments, or presidents. The apostle Paul, however, writing under the inspiration of the Holy Spirit, instructs us in Ephesians 6:12 that "our struggle is not against flesh and blood, but against the rulers, against the powers, against the world forces of this darkness, against the spiritual forces of wickedness in the heavenly places" (NASB). In the blindness of his pride and hatred, Haman surely assumed that he controlled the fate of the Jews. The invisible and almighty God, however, "who works out everything in agreement with the decision of His will" (Eph. 1:11), providentially overrules all other authorities.

*List some circumstances in our world today that appear to be beyond the control of the invisible and almighty God.*

*What ways might you respond or help direct these circumstances for good?*

## HAMAN, THE ENEMY OF GOD'S PEOPLE
### *(Esther 3:7-11)*

The Israelites had received "righteous statutes and ordinances like this entire law" (Deut. 4:8)—the law that God had given to Moses generations before Mordecai and Esther (see 4:1-8). The Persians, on the other hand, like many Ancient Near East cultures, were steeped in religious superstition and tradition. So when Haman determined that he would have the Jews exterminated, he was equally determined to make sure he selected the most fatefully appropriate day. Haman presumably had astrologers or diviners cast "Pur (that is, the lot) ... for each day in each month" (Esth. 3:7) to determine this judgment day.

The word *Pur* appears to derive from the Akkadian term *puru*, meaning *lot* or *fate*. The term didn't refer to a mystical or unguided chance outcome but rather a determined end. As we'll see, an end or a fate had indeed been determined for all involved in this plot but not by Haman.

*Why do we inherently want good to triumph in the end?*

As chief among Ahasuerus's officials, Haman exploited his knowledge of the king's desire to maintain the unity of the great Persian Empire. Haman was counting on the fact that King Ahasuerus would allow no group under his dominion to threaten that cohesion or his power as the emperor. Haman therefore singled out the Jewish people and put his own political spin on the character of this "one ethnic group, scattered throughout the peoples in every province of your kingdom" (v. 8). Weaving together a combination of truth and lies, as well as offering a contribution to the royal treasury amounting to half the annual income of the Persian Empire (see v. 9), Haman convinced King Ahasuerus that it wasn't "in the king's best interest to tolerate" this ethnic group (see v. 8) and that it had to be destroyed.

---

**KEY DOCTRINE**
*The Kingdom*

The kingdom of God includes both His general sovereignty over the universe and His particular kingship over people who willfully acknowledge Him as King. Christians ought to pray and labor that the Kingdom will come and God's will be done on earth.

Several points of interest arise here.

1. The fact that Haman possessed such persuasive influence over the king is somewhat telling of Ahasuerus's character. Ahasuerus had invaded Greece in an attempt to expand Persian dominion. The invasion didn't go well, not only ending in defeat but also sparking other rebellions in the empire. Ahasuerus's shaken confidence in his own tactical prowess may have contributed to his willingness to heed the counsel of his officials rather than, as king, lead his people with informed and wise conviction (see Prov. 29:4,12,14).

2. No indication is given that Ahasuerus inquired further about exactly who this "one ethnic group" was (Esth. 3:8). He simply authorized Haman's request to have it exterminated. Whether this abdication of due diligence was the result of Ahasuerus's propensity for Persian partying or his zeal to put down any possible sign of insurrection, the king's cold indifference to the genocide of an entire people group in his empire can't be considered anything less than demonically influenced (see 2 Cor. 10:3-5; Eph. 6:12).

3. Esther 3:11 possibly indicates that Ahasuerus—for whatever reason—didn't accept Haman's extravagant financial offer. Rather, the king simply authorized the resources necessary for Haman to execute his plan. Again, the spiritual and ethical blindness that can authorize the extermination of countless fellow human beings, without any pangs of conscience, displays the depravity of the human heart apart from the restraining grace of the invisible God (see Rom. 9:17).

4. King Ahasuerus was concerned to preserve his kingdom and authority at any cost. The irony of this feature of Esther's story will unfold in due time as we continue our study. For now, however, consider the great lengths to which both Haman and King Ahasuerus went to preserve

their own "kingdoms" and people. This mindset of self-preservation at any cost, as well as the "fate" or the outcome God determines for such a mindset, is addressed by Jesus in the New Testament (see Mark 8:35-37; Luke 9:24-25).

# HAMAN, THE SELF-CONFIDENT
## (Esther 3:15)

Under the strict "laws of Persia and Media," "a document written in the king's name and sealed with the royal signet ring cannot be revoked" (1:19; 8:8; also see Dan. 6:8,12). Haman himself had crafted the exact language of the king's edict "to destroy, kill, and annihilate all the Jewish people—young and old, women and children—and plunder their possessions on a single day, the thirteenth day of Adar [March–April], the twelfth month" (Esth. 3:13). This edict was then translated into the languages of all the peoples living in the empire and distributed from Susa by courier to governmental leaders in each of the 127 provinces. The extermination date and fate of the Jewish people had been determined.

Despite the confusion into which such an announcement had thrown the city of Susa, both "the king and Haman sat down to drink" (v. 15). That is, they both resorted to the drunken banqueting that was customary among the detached Persian aristocracy. Here again is exhibited the life-disregarding darkness of the depraved human heart apart from the restraining grace of the invisible God.

*What forces could motivate the human heart to disregard or hate others created in the image of God (see Gen. 9:6)?*

*What forces or actions could motivate the human heart to regard all human life as God does?*

**BIBLE SKILL**

**Dig deeper into the background, using a Bible dictionary (either in print or on the Internet).**

Use a Bible dictionary to learn more about Agag and the Agagites (also known as Amalekites). Look for ways their history intersected the history of God's covenant people, Israel. Seek to determine how those intersections could have impacted Haman and his view of the Jews.

# ❯ OBEY THE TEXT

God's people can bring honor to God when facing persecution and misunderstanding. Pride left unchecked opens the door to greater sin, including the evil of ethnic and religious hatred.

*How can you respond to modern-day forms of persecution toward people groups?*

*As a group, how can you encourage one another in moments of personal attack or misunderstanding?*

*What steps will you take to seek understanding and promote peace without compromising faith in God?*

## MEMORIZE

"Mordecai would not bow down or pay homage." Esther 3:2

Use the space provided to make observations and record prayer requests during the group experience for this session.

## MY THOUGHTS

Record insights and questions from the group experience.

_____
_____
_____
_____
_____
_____

## MY RESPONSE

Note specific ways you will put into practice the truth explored this week.

_____
_____
_____
_____
_____
_____

## MY PRAYERS

List specific prayer needs and answers to remember this week.

_____
_____
_____
_____
_____
_____

# GODLY SORROW AND COURAGE

Prayerful mourning can lead to faithful and selfless action.

# ❯ UNDERSTAND THE CONTEXT

USE THE FOLLOWING PAGES TO PREPARE FOR YOUR GROUP TIME.

"GIVE SORROW WORDS. THE GRIEF THAT DOES NOT SPEAK WHISPERS THE O'ER FRAUGHT HEART AND BIDS IT BREAK."
—*William Shakespeare*

Some things can't be undone. There seems to be a point of no return that people, relationships, or series of events reach, either regrettably or intentionally. There's no turning back. A word. A decision. An accident. A betrayal. A loss. A death. Finality.

Everyone in the Persian Empire understood that once the king had established a law and sealed it with his signet ring, "as a law of the Medes and Persians, it is irrevocable and cannot be changed" (Dan. 6:8; also see v. 12; Esth. 1:19; 8:8). Haman was well aware of this fact. As his cavalier return to the banqueting table clearly demonstrated, Haman was confident that his desire was about to be fulfilled: the Jews, the ancient enemy of his people, the Amalekites, were about to be annihilated once and for all. The irrevocable law of the land had now determined that fate.

Apparently, another law of the Medes and Persians had determined that no mourners could enter the palace grounds. Perhaps the motivation behind this standard was that such displays of emotion, particularly sorrow, by the king or other officials was beneath the dignity of a leader or exhibited weakness, which the people would then emulate (see 2 Sam. 3:32-34; 6:16,20). Nehemiah, who later served as a butler to King Artaxerxes (the son and successor of Ahasuerus), alluded to this custom when he wrote, "I had never been sad in [the king's] presence." Then, when questioned by the king about his visible sadness over Jerusalem's disrepair, Nehemiah expressed, "I was overwhelmed with fear" (Neh. 2:1-2).

This law was likely in force at the time of Mordecai and Esther, for when Mordecai learned of the king's edict to exterminate all Jews throughout the empire, he intentionally limited the public display of his mourning only "as far as the King's Gate" (Esth. 4:2), probably where he served as one of the king's officials. As a dignitary, Mordecai was aware that his actions might not reach the attention of the king, but he surely intended them to capture the attention of some others—most importantly, his cousin Esther.

# ❯ ESTHER 4:1-4,8-17

## Think About It

*Circle descriptions of mourning and sorrow.*

*Underline words or phrases that point to faith in God.*

**1** When Mordecai learned all that had occurred, he tore his clothes, put on sackcloth and ashes, went into the middle of the city, and cried loudly and bitterly. **2** He only went as far as the King's Gate, since the law prohibited anyone wearing sackcloth from entering the King's Gate. **3** There was great mourning among the Jewish people in every province where the king's command and edict came. They fasted, wept, and lamented, and many lay on sackcloth and ashes. **4** Esther's female servants and her eunuchs came and reported the news to her, and the queen was overcome with fear. She sent clothes for Mordecai to wear so he could take off his sackcloth, but he did not accept them.

**8** Mordecai also gave him a copy of the written decree issued in Susa ordering their destruction, so that Hathach might show it to Esther, explain it to her, and command her to approach the king, implore his favor, and plead with him personally for her people. **9** Hathach came and repeated Mordecai's response to Esther. **10** Esther spoke to Hathach and commanded him to tell Mordecai, **11** "All the royal officials and the people of the royal provinces know that one law applies to every man or woman who approaches the king in the inner courtyard and who has not been summoned—the death penalty. Only if the king extends the gold scepter will that person live. I have not been summoned to appear before the king for the last 30 days." **12** Esther's response was reported to Mordecai. **13** Mordecai told the messenger to reply to Esther, "Don't think that you will escape the fate of all the Jews because you are in the king's palace. **14** If you keep silent at this time, liberation and deliverance will come to the Jewish people from another place, but you and your father's house will be destroyed. Who knows, perhaps you have come to your royal position for such a time as this." **15** Esther sent this reply to Mordecai: **16** "Go and assemble all the Jews who can be found in Susa and fast for me. Don't eat or drink for three days, day or night. I and my female servants will also fast in the same way. After that, I will go to the king even if it is against the law. If I perish, I perish." **17** So Mordecai went and did everything Esther had ordered him.

# › EXPLORE THE TEXT

## MORDECAI'S TORN SOUL *(Esther 4:1-4)*

On hearing the tragic and irrevocable news that all Jews everywhere were to be exterminated, Mordecai—one of the king's officials and now known to be a Jew himself (see 3:4)—expressed both his grief and his prayers to God in a manner customary to Jews and other ancient peoples: "he tore his clothes, put on sackcloth and ashes, went into the middle of the city, and cried loudly and bitterly" (4:1; also see Gen. 37:34; 2 Sam. 3:31; Isa. 37:1; Jonah 3:5-8). Mordecai was joined by other Jews both in Susa and in every province in this public mourning of their impending fate.

*When was the last time you experienced intense sadness? For what did you mourn? How did you express your sorrow?*

Tearing one's clothing and donning coarse burlap and dust or ashes to display grief may appear a bit sensational to sophisticated 21st-century Westerners. However, that's precisely the point of such a display. Those who mourned this way were expressing emphatic grief over a circumstance of inexpressible sorrow or injustice. Such mourners were so undone by the circumstance that their own lives and reputations were the least of their concerns. Moreover, the mourners considered their own souls ripped apart, very much like their torn garments. In baring their souls to plead for help before an almighty, holy Deity, mourners recognized the unworthy and earthbound state of their own beings in the presence of God. Only covering themselves in unsightly, uncomfortable clothing and dust or ashes could express the brokenness and humility the mourners felt.

On hearing about this exhibition by Mordecai, Esther "was overcome with fear" (Esth. 4:4) even before she understood "what he was doing and why" (v. 5). The Hebrew term *chil*, which was used to describe Esther's response, was often used in the context of childbirth. Esther's emotional distress, therefore, could be translated, "She writhed in anguish."

The fears that any of us might expect surely flooded Esther's mind. Mordecai was evidently a sober-minded man, so Esther would have assumed that such a display of indignity wasn't without serious reason. Moreover, Esther may have feared for both Mordecai's and her own safety, since this respected

king's official and her own adoptive father may well have been risking his life by expressing grief so vehemently just outside the gate where he served and near where such mourning was prohibited. Her response, whether motivated by fear or genuinely intended to comfort, was to send clothes to replace the sackcloth—an offer that was rejected by Mordecai. His sorrow needed to be expressed. It was worthy of feeling the weight of its severity—severity he needed Esther to grasp. She needed to be disturbed and stirred to action.

*When have you tried to rush, cover up, or comfort someone in their sorrow in a way that wasn't helpful? Was your desire really to help them or to feel better or more comfortable yourself?*

## MORDECAI'S CHALLENGE TO THE QUEEN *(Esther 4:8-14)*

Mordecai's display had been successful in capturing the attention of his cousin, the queen. Interestingly, Esther discovered the news of the king's edict as a result of Mordecai's public response to the edict rather than from the king's direct communication with her (see vv. 4-5). Much insight can be gleaned about the level of communication between the king and queen of Persia, considering the fact that Mordecai's exhibition was the means by which the queen discovered the news of the king's edict and that the queen had not been invited to appear before the king for the prior 30 days (see v. 11).

Esther dispatched her trusted attendant, Hathach (whose name possibly means *courier)*, to find out why Mordecai was behaving this way. Despite any apprehension Hathach may have had in delivering such a forceful message to his queen, Hathach relayed the full details of

Mordecai's instruction to "command her to approach the king, implore his favor, and plead with him personally for her people" (v. 8). Mordecai was aware not only that his familiarity with his adopted daughter would grant him an audience with her but also that no option could be excluded, because the fate of his and Esther's people was at stake.

*When have you had to communicate hard truth to someone? How did you do so?*

*When have you received bad news? How did you respond?*

Esther considered her response to Mordecai and reminded him of another law of the Medes and Persians: anyone—even the queen—who approached the king without being summoned by him was risking his or her own life (see v. 11). Only the king himself could grant clemency to someone so presumptuous. Mordecai, again fully aware that all options must be on the table, counseled Esther from the standpoint of his seasoned wisdom as one committed to the law, promises, and providence of the God of Israel, as well as his years of experience as a royal official. With probably the most important and memorable words in the entire Book of Esther, Mordecai reminded his young Jewish cousin of both the faithfulness of the God of Israel and her own corresponding responsibility to be faithful as someone in covenant relationship with God. Mordecai challenged Esther:

> *Don't think that you will escape the fate of all the Jews because you are in the king's palace. If you keep silent at this time, liberation and deliverance will come to the Jewish people from another place, but you and your father's house will be destroyed. Who knows, perhaps you have come to your royal position for such a time as this.* **Esther 4:13-14**

The phrase "for such a time as this" (v. 14) showcases the Book of Esther's theme of the invisible God's providence over all things. The English word *providence* comes from two Latin terms, *pro* and *videre*, meaning *to see before* or *foresight*. Mordecai's challenge to Esther, as well as to all who would read her story afterward, was to trust that the invisible God, the God of Israel, sees all things beforehand and governs all things according to His wise and good purposes, including the salvation of all those who love Him (see Rom. 8:28; Eph. 1:11).

*Describe a time when you experienced a dilemma-of-faith situation in which the risks of action were high. Who or what helped you decide how to proceed?*

*When have you sensed God positioning you at just the right place and time to do something for His glory?*

*Who within your sphere of influence needs encouragement to grow in faith and obedience, and how can you offer encouragement in a God-honoring way?*

# MORDECAI'S PRAYER WITH THE QUEEN
## (Esther 4:15-17)

Elsewhere in Scripture, Abraham, another individual living among different cultures, is presented as the father of all who possess the kind of faith that pleases God. The apostle Paul wrote that Abraham believed God, and God counted it to him as righteousness (see Rom. 4:12,16-22). Abraham's faith may appear radical, but faith, by definition, is simply believing that what God has said is true. Abraham so firmly believed God's promise of offspring "as numerous as ... the sand on the seashore" (Gen. 22:17) that he was willing—at God's clear command—to sacrifice the only son through whom God's promise was to be fulfilled (see Gen. 22:1-18). Abraham believed that even if he put Isaac to death, God was able to raise him from the dead in order to keep His promise (see Heb. 11:19).

Faith that pleases God, therefore, follows "in the footsteps of the faith our father Abraham had while he was still uncircumcised" (Rom. 4:12; also see Matt. 17:20; Heb. 11:6). People like Esther who exercise this kind of faith trust God's providence and promises even more than they value their own lives. Confronted with a challenge to respond in faith, Esther exercised the kind of faith that demonstrated that she was an offspring of her father Abraham. Esther requested Mordecai to assemble all the Jews who could be found in Susa, and then she convened a corporate fast to seek the invisible God's intervention. Following "in the footsteps of the faith our father Abraham had" (Rom. 4:12), Esther courageously determined, "I will go to the king even if it is against the law. If I perish, I perish" (Esth. 4:16).

*How are you challenged to trust God with your circumstances—however tragic—as Esther trusted God with the faith of Abraham?*

**BIBLE SKILL**
**Compare another instance of an activity in Scripture, looking for commonalities and differences.**

Esther called for a fast to be instituted as she prepared to approach the king. Compare other Bible passages in which fasting was called for (examples: Acts 13:1-2; 14:21-23).

*How are the purposes of fasting similar and different in these passages?*

*What role can fasting have in the lives of Christians today?*

*When have you engaged in spiritual disciplines such as prayer and fasting for courage to do something God wants you to do? What was the result?*

# ❯ OBEY THE TEXT

The effects of sin in this world are tragic. As believers, we have the responsibility to act on the truth of God that He makes known to us. Obedience can involve risk, but no risk is as great as failing to obey. We can take action in light of God's providence, leaving the results to Him.

*Take time right now to feel the burden of sin's effect on this world. Express your heart to God.*

*From what, with whom, and when will you fast and pray specifically for clarity and boldness about God's will for your life?*

*List the risks involved when you hesitate to act on something God directs you to do. What steps will you take to be obedient?*

*In what situations have you tried to control the outcome instead of trusting the results to God? What steps will you take to relinquish control and trust God completely?*

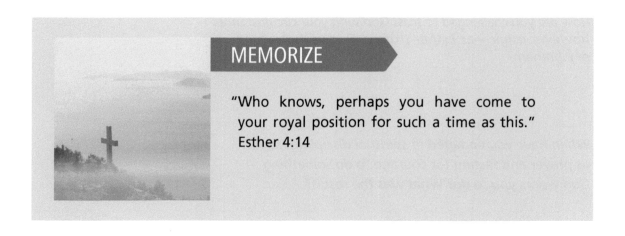

## MEMORIZE ❯

"Who knows, perhaps you have come to your royal position for such a time as this."
Esther 4:14

Use the space provided to make observations and record prayer requests during the group experience for this session.

## MY THOUGHTS

Record insights and questions from the group experience.

_____

_____

_____

_____

_____

_____

## MY RESPONSE

Note specific ways you will put into practice the truth explored this week.

_____

_____

_____

_____

_____

_____

## MY PRAYERS

List specific prayer needs and answers to remember this week.

_____

_____

_____

_____

_____

_____

# SELFLESS OR SELFISH LIVING

God raises up mediators to intercede for His people facing dangerous opposition.

# >> UNDERSTAND THE CONTEXT

USE THE FOLLOWING PAGES TO PREPARE FOR YOUR GROUP TIME.

Great freedom and boldness come with knowing that life isn't about us. Living for the approval of others or for the protection and advancement of ourselves becomes an empty, endless pursuit. Ironically, life is rich with meaning when we live sacrificially for the sake of others.

John Woolman, an 18th-century American Quaker, dedicated his adult life to the cause of abolishing slavery in colonial America. Woolman possessed such moral power and influence—especially among his fellow Quakers—that he convinced many slaveholders to free their slaves. In doing so, Woolman demonstrated the power of one person, under God, to stand for what is right.

The impetus of Woolman's example came straight from Scripture. The Bible is filled with accounts of men and women who trusted in God and took courageous stands to live for Him. Some of them faced the fearful prospect of martyrdom, yet they didn't back down from their devotion to the living God. God used these men and women—individuals like Esther—to advance His kingdom purposes.

Dangerous times call for courageous stands. Mordecai suggested to Esther that she was born for such a time as the Jews faced under Ahasuerus. God had made her aware of a great need and positioned her to take action, interceding for His covenant people. She had a choice to make. Would she live for her own temporary comfort or for the well-being of others? Would she risk her own life to oppose a vicious and selfish enemy, under the threat of an unchangeable law, and risk being misunderstood by a king who had rid himself of his previous queen for disrespecting him? Esther's only hope was to break all expectations and cultural norms. The lives of God's people hung in the balance.

"BEHIND EVERY SPECIFIC CALL, WHETHER IT IS TO TEACH OR PREACH OR WRITE OR ENCOURAGE OR COMFORT, THERE IS A DEEPER CALL THAT GIVES SHAPE TO THE FIRST: THE CALL TO GIVE OURSELVES AWAY—THE CALL TO DIE."
—*Michael Card*

# ESTHER 5:1-10,14

## Think About It

Circle words expressing emotions in this passage: approval, pleases, joy, fear, rage, and so on.

What do these words emphasize about Esther's mindset?

What do they emphasize about Haman's mindset?

**1** On the third day, Esther dressed up in her royal clothing and stood in the inner courtyard of the palace facing it. The king was sitting on his royal throne in the royal courtroom, facing its entrance. **2** As soon as the king saw Queen Esther standing in the courtyard, she won his approval. The king extended the gold scepter in his hand toward Esther, and she approached and touched the tip of the scepter. **3** "What is it, Queen Esther?" the king asked her. "Whatever you want, even to half the kingdom, will be given to you." **4** "If it pleases the king," Esther replied, "may the king and Haman come today to the banquet I have prepared for them." **5** The king commanded, "Hurry, and get Haman so we can do as Esther has requested." So the king and Haman went to the banquet Esther had prepared. **6** While drinking the wine, the king asked Esther, "Whatever you ask will be given to you. Whatever you want, even to half the kingdom, will be done." **7** Esther answered, "This is my petition and my request: **8** If the king approves of me and if it pleases the king to grant my petition and perform my request, may the king and Haman come to the banquet I will prepare for them. Tomorrow I will do what the king has asked." **9** That day Haman left full of joy and in good spirits. But when Haman saw Mordecai at the King's Gate, and Mordecai didn't rise or tremble in fear at his presence, Haman was filled with rage toward Mordecai. **10** Yet Haman controlled himself and went home. He sent for his friends and his wife Zeresh to join him.

**14** His wife Zeresh and all his friends told him, "Have them build a gallows 75 feet high. Ask the king in the morning to hang Mordecai on it. Then go to the banquet with the king and enjoy yourself." The advice pleased Haman, so he had the gallows constructed.

# ❯ EXPLORE THE TEXT

## ESTHER'S FAITHFUL ACT *(Esther 5:1-5)*

As we have seen, the laws of the Medes and Persians were very specific. One such law prevented anyone from approaching the king whom he hadn't summoned. Perhaps this prohibition was due to the Persian Empire's long history of political assassinations. (In fact, Ahasuerus was murdered in his own bed less than 10 years later by the commander of his royal bodyguard, Artabanus, who, on discovery, was executed along with his sons by Ahasuerus's son and successor, Artaxerxes I.) This prohibition to approach the king, no doubt, also bolstered the king's authoritative reputation.

The king's counselors had encouraged the reinforcement of this authoritative posture in light of Vashti's public challenge to the king's authority (see 1:13-22). Esther surely considered her predecessor's misstep—and demise—as she contemplated her own dilemma. Despite the danger of either her action or her inaction, Esther was compelled to make the very difficult decision to risk her life and approach her husband, the king, uninvited and to trust God with the outcome.

Some suggest that because Esther had "not been summoned to appear before the king for the last 30 days" (4:11), she had fallen out of his favor. Though that possibility exists, no evidence is presented to support the theory. Considering that (1) Ahasuerus was involved in constant political and military enterprises; (2) like many Ancient Near East cultures, Persian kings maintained harems; and (3) Ancient Near East marital relationships don't necessarily parallel 21st-century Western notions of mutually submissive partnerships, perhaps no more is suggested by the separation than that the king simply had no opportunity for the kind of engagement with Esther that he had during his initial pursuit and enthronement of his new queen. Further, the king's immediate response to Esther on her approach suggests that she hadn't fallen out of favor with him (see 5:2).

*In what issues, relationships, or situations do you currently risk being misunderstood or unintentionally offending someone with your faith? In what areas of your life could there be great personal cost for taking a stand or speaking up for what's right?*

Having determined to approach the king "against the law" (4:16), Esther prayed and fasted for three days with Mordecai, her female servants, and all the willing Jews who were found in Susa. The consistent grace of character that had always won Esther "favor" and "approval in the sight of everyone who saw her" (2:9,15; also see 2:17) also adorned her approach to the land's chief dignitary, even though he was her husband. Esther's prudence, reverence, and humility as she prepared to enter the presence of the king—who literally held in his hand the power of life and death for Esther—is reminiscent of the approach to God commended by Solomon in Ecclesiastes 5:1-2. Esther adorned herself in a manner befitting an audience with the king of the empire, entered his gates, stood in his courtyard, and humbly awaited the king's word. "As soon as the king saw Queen Esther standing in the courtyard, she won his approval" such that he was willing to offer her "even to half the kingdom" (Esth. 5:2-3,6; also see Luke 12:32; John 16:23-24).

Esther's faith is demonstrated in part by her considering the life of others more important than her own (see John 15:13; Phil. 2.3). We may not be able to make a definitive statement about Esther's faith based only on the fact that she had prepared a banquet even before she was sure she would be alive to attend it. Even though Esther was walking "in the footsteps of the faith our father Abraham had" (Rom. 4:12), she had no sure reason to believe her life would somehow be spared. Abraham, believing God's promise (Heb. 11:19), with similar forethought, told the young men accompanying him to Mount Moriah, where he would sacrifice Isaac, "Stay here with the donkey. The boy and I will go over there to worship; then we'll come back to you" (Gen. 22:5). Esther's forethought, however, does exhibit her hope and readiness in the event that her approach and request were received.

*When have you had to act before you knew what God was going to do?*

The banquet Esther had prepared was for her husband and his chief adviser, Haman. The text provides no insight about Esther's reason for inviting Haman. Whatever her motivation, Esther was seeking an opportunity to expose Haman and his evil scheme and to plead for the lives of her people. She patiently waited on the Lord (see Ps. 40:1) instead of emotionally forcing her desires.

*When have you had to wait patiently, when perhaps not saying or doing anything in the moment was harder or scarier than trying to take matters into your own hands?*

## ESTHER'S HUMBLE PETITION
### (Esther 5:6-10)

At the banquet, "while drinking the wine" (v. 6)—much as the king had been doing when he commanded Vashti to be paraded before his guests (see 1:7-11; Dan. 5:1-4)—he told Esther once again that her request was his command (see Esth. 5:6). Clearly, Esther continued to hold the king's "favor and approval" (2:17), whether by God's providence, Esther's character and beauty, or both.

Just as the text provides no explanation for why Esther wanted Haman at the banquet, no motivation is given for Esther's postponing her request until a second day of banqueting (see 5:8). Given Esther's humility and temperance (see 2:13,15b), perhaps the initial banquet was either customary or prudent. Similarly, in light of the Persian propensity for banqueting, another reason may be that such proposals were customarily conducted after the guests had been sufficiently charmed by food, drink, and other creature comforts (see 1:5-10a). Another option may be that Esther was prayerfully attempting to discern the king's receptivity to her proposal. She had not yet determined how to broach the subject with her husband and was waiting for just the right opportunity to submit the matter to him. Whatever Esther's motivation for withholding her request until a second banquet, the invisible God was ordering Esther's steps with perfect timing.

**KEY DOCTRINE**
*Christian Justice*

All Christians are obligated to seek to make the will of Christ supreme in their lives and in society. Believers should work to provide for the orphaned, the needy, the abused, the aged, the helpless, and the sick, contending for the sanctity of human life from conception to natural death. Every Christian should seek to bring industry, government, and society as a whole under the sway of the principles of righteousness, truth, and brotherly love.

Before the sun set on the first day, Haman's pride had inflated even more than before, having been invited as the guest of honor to not one but two days of banqueting with hosts who could reasonably be considered the king and the queen of the world. He left the palace "full of joy and in good spirits" (5:9). As he left, he passed by Mordecai at the King's Gate, who, not the slightest bit intimidated by Haman, still refused to bow in his presence. Haman's pride filled him with rage toward Mordecai, though he maintained his composure as he passed. On arriving at home, Haman summoned his friends and his wife and proceeded to boast about the glory, favor, and approval the king had extended to him (see vv. 10-12).

*When has your own wounded pride caused you to desire or even seek someone else's removal, misfortune, or even harm?*

*When have you sought bad counsel to affirm your overly emotional desires?*

*When have you acted rashly with pride, jealousy, anger, or ambition?*

# HAMAN'S FAITHLESS PRIDE
## (Esther 5:14)

Still discontented that Mordecai even had a place at the King's Gate, Haman listened to the counsel of his wife and friends, to whom he had just boasted about himself and all his accomplishments. They counseled Haman to have a seven-story gallows built and then ask the king to hang Mordecai on it in the morning. They urged Haman, "Then go to the banquet with the king and enjoy yourself" (v. 14). We're told that this advice "pleased Haman" (v. 14).

As we saw in Esther 3:7-11 (session 2), this is another portrait of the depravity of the human heart apart from the restraining grace of the invisible God. Haman's spiritual and ethical blindness was displayed by the fact that he could be pleased with advice to put to death another human being made in the image of God merely because of his personal disregard for that person.

*When have you given someone ungodly advice, seeking to affirm their emotions and desires?*

*How are you like Haman?*

*Read Matthew 5:21-22. What did Jesus teach about evil deeds and the condition of our hearts?*

**BIBLE SKILL**
**Search for other places a word is used in Scripture.**

Use the concordance at the back of your Bible or search online* for the following words from today's passage and write any key insights on what the Bible says about each. To dig even deeper, also look up synonyms and antonyms.

*Joy*

*Rage*

*mywsb.com is a great free resource.

# ❯OBEY THE TEXT

God works behind the scenes, so to speak, but He also works through His people. He acts through our actions. He works in our work.

*Of what need(s) are you aware?*

*What do you need to do for the sake of God's work in the world around you, no matter what the potential personal sacrifice?*

*What has kept you from fully giving yourself to meet that need? What intimidates or scares you?*

*What steps will you take to share the love, hope, and salvation of Jesus regarding that need?*

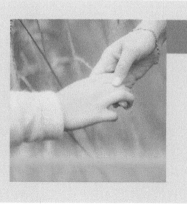

## MEMORIZE

"The LORD said: I will certainly set you free and care for you. I will certainly intercede for you in a time of trouble, in your time of distress, with the enemy." Jeremiah 15:11

Use the space provided to make observations and record prayer requests during the group experience for this session.

## MY THOUGHTS

Record insights and questions from the group experience.

_____
_____
_____
_____
_____
_____
_____

## MY RESPONSE

Note specific ways you will put into practice the truth explored this week.

_____
_____
_____
_____
_____
_____
_____

## MY PRAYERS

List specific prayer needs and answers to remember this week.

_____
_____
_____
_____
_____
_____
_____

# GOD'S PERFECT TIMING

God will ultimately bring justice to the wicked and grace to His people.

# ❯ UNDERSTAND THE CONTEXT

USE THE FOLLOWING PAGES TO PREPARE FOR YOUR GROUP TIME.

Everybody loves a good plot twist. A great story has an audience hanging on the edge of their seats and then catches everyone by surprise with something they never saw coming. Rags to riches, star-crossed lovers, underdogs—there's nothing quite like a tale of unexpected fate. Perhaps no story is as full of irony and suspense as the Book of Esther—one that only the brilliant Author of life could have scripted.

As the story of Esther unfolds and the plot thickens, the scene now moves from the royal banquet hall to the king's bedchamber. Esther's first banquet had concluded, but the tension in the story remains because her weighty concern hadn't yet been addressed; her people were still in peril. Haman, the king's chief adviser, still despised Mordecai and was planning his execution the next morning. The date was still set for the slaughter of the Jewish people.

As "fate" or Pur would have it (see Esth. 3:7)—that is, as the invisible God determined circumstances and their outcomes—you may recall that Mordecai had exposed a plot on the king's life. Fortunately—rather, providentially—"this event was recorded in the Historical Record in the king's presence" (2:23). Like a good storyteller, the writer of the Book of Esther didn't neglect to note this seemingly insignificant detail earlier in the story, precisely because it isn't at all insignificant in the invisible God's greater story.

***What seemingly insignificant detail in your own story turned out to be a significant factor in your life?***

***How has the relationship between those circumstances and their outcomes directed you to see God's hand in them?***

> "EVEN WHEN THINGS SEEM TO BE GOING WRONG, THEY JUST COULD BE GOING RIGHT BECAUSE WHEN YOU'RE IN GOD'S WILL, THE NEGATIVES ARE PART OF HIS POSITIVE PROGRAM."
> —*Dr. Tony Evans*

# ❯ ESTHER 6:1-3,6-11; 7:1-6,10; 8:1-2

## Think About It

*Circle apparent irony revealing God's providence.*

*List any reversals of fate, good timing, or instances of being in the right place at the right time in the story of Esther so far.*

**6:1** That night sleep escaped the king, so he ordered the book recording daily events to be brought and read to the king. **2** They found the written report of how Mordecai had informed on Bigthana and Teresh, two eunuchs who guarded the king's entrance, when they planned to assassinate King Ahasuerus. **3** The king inquired, "What honor and special recognition have been given to Mordecai for this act?" The king's personal attendants replied, "Nothing has been done for him." **6** Haman entered, and the king asked him, "What should be done for the man the king wants to honor?" Haman thought to himself, "Who is it the king would want to honor more than me?" **7** Haman told the king, "For the man the king wants to honor: **8** Have them bring a royal garment that the king himself has worn and a horse the king himself has ridden, which has a royal diadem on its head. **9** Put the garment and the horse under the charge of one of the king's most noble officials. Have them clothe the man the king wants to honor, parade him on the horse through the city square, and proclaim before him, 'This is what is done for the man the king wants to honor.' " **10** The king told Haman, "Hurry, and do just as you proposed. Take a garment and a horse for Mordecai the Jew, who is sitting at the King's Gate. Do not leave out anything you have suggested." **11** So Haman took the garment and the horse. He clothed Mordecai and paraded him through the city square, crying out before him, "This is what is done for the man the king wants to honor."

**7:1** The king and Haman came to feast with Esther the queen. **2** Once again, on the second day while drinking wine, the king asked Esther, "Queen Esther, whatever you ask will be given to you. Whatever you seek, even to half the kingdom, will be done." **3** Queen Esther answered, "If I have obtained your approval, my king, and if the king is pleased, spare my life—this is my request; and spare my people—this is my desire. **4** For my people and I have been sold out to destruction, death, and extermination. If we had merely been sold as male and female slaves, I would have kept silent. Indeed, the trouble wouldn't be worth burdening the king." **5** King Ahasuerus spoke up and asked Queen Esther, "Who is this, and where is the one who would devise such a scheme?" **6** Esther answered, "The adversary and enemy is this evil Haman." Haman stood terrified before the king and queen. **10** They hanged Haman on the gallows he had prepared for Mordecai. Then the king's anger subsided.

**8:1** That same day King Ahasuerus awarded Queen Esther the estate of Haman, the enemy of the Jews. Mordecai entered the king's presence because Esther had revealed her relationship to Mordecai. **2** The king removed his signet ring he had recovered from Haman and gave it to Mordecai, and Esther put him in charge of Haman's estate.

# ❯ EXPLORE THE TEXT

## *THE KING'S SLEEPLESS NIGHT*
### *(Esther 6:1-3)*

On the night of Esther's initial banquet, the king couldn't sleep. Neither the earthly writer nor the divine Author of the Book of Esther saw fit to include the reason. It's important to note the role of the invisible God in causing the king's insomnia. The Septuagint (the Greek translation of the Hebrew Old Testament) emphasizes God's activity in Ahasuerus's sleeplessness. It translates the first half of verse 1, "The Lord removed sleep from the king that night." The translators of the Septuagint may well have had in mind Daniel 2:1, which says "sleep deserted" King Nebuchadnezzar due to the dreams God gave him. Daniel informed his king that the same "God in heaven who reveals mysteries" (2:28) had revealed the king's dreams and their interpretation to Daniel "in a vision at night" (2:19; also see vv. 28-30). These texts communicate the role of the omnipotent God even in the sleep or sleeplessness of these pagan kings.

While awake, King Ahasuerus decided to occupy the time by familiarizing himself with events as recorded in what might be called the Persian Royal Chronicle. Again, as God's providence would have it, Ahasuerus came across "the written report of how Mordecai had informed on Bigthana and Teresh, two eunuchs who guarded the king's entrance, when they planned to assassinate King Ahasuerus" (Esth. 6:2; also see 2:21-23). The king summoned his personal attendants to ask them what had been done to reward Mordecai for his loyal act. When he discovered that nothing had been done, the king determined to remedy that oversight.

Was it mere coincidence that the sleepless Ahasuerus made this discovery at the very moment Haman had entered the king's court to ask the king to execute Mordecai (see 6:4-5)? Was it coincidence that Haman's wife and friends had counseled him only moments earlier to make such a request? Was it mere coincidence that rewarding Mordecai for an act of integrity he had done some time ago had been overlooked until just such a time as this?

The writer of the Book of Esther was conveying the point that although circumstances may appear to be caused by "fate," determined by an earthly power, the sovereign God alone orders His universe as He sees fit:

> *... declaring the end from the beginning*
>
>> *and from ancient times things not yet done,*
>
> *saying, "My counsel shall stand,*
>
>> *and I will accomplish all my purpose."* **Isaiah 46:10, ESV**

**How can confidence in God's sovereignty govern our anxieties and actions about circumstances on our own world stage?**

## THE KING'S IRONIC COMMENDATION *(Esther 6:6-11)*

The wisdom of Solomon had already communicated to Israel the principle:

> *Pride comes before destruction,*
>
> *and an arrogant spirit before a fall.* **Proverbs 16:18**

Haman's political maneuvering had acquired for him in "a higher position than all the other officials" (Esth. 3:1). He had acquired "glorious wealth and ... many sons" (5:11). Haman's view of the situation was "Queen Esther invited no one but me to join the king at the banquet she had prepared. I am invited again tomorrow to join her with the king" (v. 12). Rather than humbling himself with gratitude for the many benefits bestowed on him, Haman allowed his pride and self-assurance to taint his understanding of the state of affairs.

Blinded to God's view of circumstances, when Haman was summoned from the king's courtyard, in his self-absorption Haman assumed the king's interests involved him. So when the king asked Haman, "What should be done for the man the king wants to honor?" (6:6) Haman unwittingly laid out the details of a most charitable honor, which he arrogantly assumed should be his own lot (see vv. 7-9). Ironically, and as divine providence would have it, the king bestowed the honor Haman had described on one far more worthy of recognition than Haman. To Haman's deep dismay, the king commanded Haman to confer the honor—to the last detail—on the last person on whom Haman would desire to bestow such honor, the very enemy he was just about to propose that the king execute, Mordecai (see vv. 10-11).

A saying of Jesus finds clear fulfillment in the story's characters Haman and Mordecai: "Whoever exalts himself will be humbled, and whoever humbles himself will be exalted" (Matt. 23:12; also see Dan. 4:37; Phil. 2:8-9; Jas. 4:6).

**KEY DOCTRINE**
*God*

There is one and only one living and true God. He is the Creator, Redeemer, Preserver, and Ruler of the universe. He is infinite in holiness, all powerful, and all knowing.

## THE KING'S PACIFIED ANGER
### (Esther 7:1-6,10)

The king's favor and approval toward Esther hadn't at all waned by the second day of banqueting. The king again asked Esther what her request was, and for a third time Ahasuerus assured Esther that his generosity toward his queen extended "even to half the kingdom" (v. 2; also see 5:3,6). That the author mentioned this expression three times is no coincidence. Repetition in Hebrew and Greek literature was often used to communicate emphasis. The repetition of an idea three times usually emphasized the definitive nature of the matter. For example, in 1 Kings 18:34, as Elijah was challenging the false prophets of Baal, he had the burnt offering and the wood on the altar of the Lord drenched in water three times, so that "the water ran around the altar and filled the trench also with water" (v. 35, ESV). Elijah (and the writer of 1 Kings) desired to assure the people that the altar was completely saturated before "the fire of the LORD fell and consumed the burnt offering and the wood and the stones and the dust, and licked up the water that was in the trench" (v. 38, ESV). In the same way, the writer of the Book of Esther intended to show the king's complete commitment to favor, approval, and generosity toward Esther.

This disposition of the king toward the humble and temperate Esther was markedly different from his anger and fury toward the defiant Vashti (see Esth. 1:12). To be sure, the circumstances between the two relationships were quite different, but fateful ordering of circumstances is precisely the point of the Book of Esther.

*What role does our own behavior play in the ways people interact with us?*

Having been assured of the king's favor, Queen Esther candidly laid her dilemma before the king, wisely and humbly framing her plea so as not to indict the king for authorizing Haman's heinous scheme. Esther stated that she and her people had been "sold out to destruction, death, and extermination" (7:4). The one who sold out Esther wasn't the king but Haman. Esther further displayed astonishing humility and temperance by communicating that "the trouble wouldn't be worth burdening the king" if the scheme merely resulted in enslavement of her people rather than genocide (v. 4).

The king was angered—to say the least—that someone "would devise such a scheme" (v. 5) against the object of his affection and her entire people. When "this evil Haman" (v. 6) was exposed as the plot's perpetrator, the shocked king dismissed himself from the banquet table, perhaps to try to make sense of the allegation, to summon executioners, or both. On his return to the banquet,

the king's eyes beheld an even more unbelievable scene: "Haman was falling on the couch where Esther was reclining" (v. 8). As providence would have it, the king misinterpreted Haman's actions, assuming Haman was attempting to "actually violate the queen while [the king was] in the palace" (v. 8). The sight was enough to resolve the matter for the now fully enraged king, and the executioners covered the head of the one whose face had become such a disgrace that it needed to be hidden from sight until he could be executed.

As providence would have it, the gallows Haman had constructed for Mordecai's execution was primed for his own. The king commanded, "Hang him on it" (v. 9). When Haman had been hanged, "the king's anger subsided" (v. 10).

## THE KING'S POETIC JUSTICE
### (Esther 8:1-2)

The truth of Proverbs 16:18 rings loudly in both the pride and catastrophic fall of Haman. His political maneuvering (see Esth. 3:1-2; 5:11b), his boasting of "his glorious wealth" (5:11), and his high-minded self-image (see 6:6-9) all amount to less than nothing, considering the loss of his life and soul (see Matt. 16:26). What's more, the lavish providence of the invisible God moved the heart of King Ahasuerus to award Queen Esther "the estate of Haman, the enemy of the Jews" (Esth. 8:1). Esther, in turn, disclosed her relationship to Mordecai, whom the king subsequently entrusted with all the authority vested in the king's own signet ring, which he had retrieved from Haman's hand. Queen Esther then transferred to Mordecai all the glorious wealth that had belonged to Haman (see vv. 1-2).

The invisible God is King in the ultimate sense. He providentially orders circumstances to "accomplish all [His] purpose" (Isa. 46:10, ESV). In the account of Esther and Mordecai, the Sovereign King rendered poetic justice to the enemy of His covenant people through the agency of the earthly king of the world-dominating Persian Empire. In this truest sense, God alone is worthy of the title King of kings and Lord of lords (see 1 Tim. 6:15; Rev. 17:14; 19:16).

> **BIBLE SKILL**
> **Examine the life and teaching of Jesus.**
>
> Jesus used contrast and irony to reveal surprising truths about the kingdom of God.
>
> *Write a short summary of each passage.*
>
> *Matthew 23:12*
>
> *Mark 10:31*
>
> *Luke 6:20-38*
>
> *John 13:1-20*

# ❯ OBEY THE TEXT

Faith takes action. What you know and believe about God becomes a life-changing reality when you step out in faith and experience Him firsthand.

*Identify areas of pride in your life. Confess them and repent, asking for God's mercy.*

*How will you guard against arrogance, entitlement, and the eventual consequences of a self-centered life?*

*What steps will you take to trust God this week and keep Him at the center of your life?*

*Identify friends who may be heading for a fall and ways you can boldly but respectfully confront them before it's too late.*

## MEMORIZE

"Pride comes before destruction, and an arrogant spirit before a fall."
Proverbs 16:18

Use the space provided to make observations and record prayer requests during the group experience for this session.

## MY THOUGHTS

Record insights and questions from the group experience.

_____

_____

_____

_____

_____

_____

## MY RESPONSE

Note specific ways you will put into practice the truth explored this week.

_____

_____

_____

_____

_____

_____

## MY PRAYERS

List specific prayer needs and answers to remember this week.

_____

_____

_____

_____

_____

_____

# LEAVING A LEGACY

The good news of salvation is worth celebrating and should be intentionally passed on to every generation.

# ❯ UNDERSTAND THE CONTEXT

There is nothing greater in this world than knowing that your life was given fully to God for His purposes and that other people know the joy of His salvation.

Two of the story's important characters have now exited stage right, as it were. The deposed first lady, Vashti, has been replaced by "another woman who is more worthy than she" (Esth. 1:19). The rise and fall of the evil Haman (see 7:6) has ended in his execution on the very gallows he had built for Mordecai's execution. Now the story turns to the Pur or fate of the Jewish people.

"In the name of King Ahasuerus and sealed with the royal signet ring," Haman had commanded the exact language of the edict "to destroy, kill, and annihilate all the Jewish people—young and old, women and children—and plunder their possessions on a single day, the thirteenth day of Adar [February–March], the twelfth month" (3:12-13). "As a law of the Medes and Persians, it is irrevocable and cannot be changed" (Dan. 6:8; also see v. 12; Esth. 1:19; 8:8).

> "LEGACY IS MUCH MORE THAN SIMPLY PASSING ON THE FAMILY NAME. LEGACY INVOLVES PASSING ON A KINGDOM WORLDVIEW AND PERSPECTIVE."
> —*Dr. Tony Evans*

Even though the perpetrator of the scheme was now dead; even though the king's favor now extended not only to Esther but also to her adoptive father, Mordecai; and even though Mordecai—in place of Haman—had been promoted in rank above all the other royal staff (see 8:2,8,10; 9:3-4; 10:3), what could be done to save God's covenant people under such seemingly inescapable circumstances? The epilogue of Esther's story unfolds so great a salvation.

*What do you think you are currently known for and as?*

*How do you want to be remembered?*

"n though
st out un
e the he
them fr
ng them
have ch
here.

# ⮞ ESTHER 8:3-5,8,11,15-17; 9:1,20-23; 10:3

## Think About It

*Underline words that express negative emotions, actions, people, or situations.*

*Circle words that express positive emotions, actions, or situations.*

**8:3** Esther addressed the king again. She fell at his feet, wept, and begged him to revoke the evil of Haman the Agagite, and his plot he had devised against the Jews. **4** The king extended the gold scepter toward Esther, so she got up and stood before the king. **5** She said, "If it pleases the king, and I have found approval before him, if the matter seems right to the king and I am pleasing in his sight, let a royal edict be written. Let it revoke the documents the scheming Haman son of Hammedatha the Agagite, wrote to destroy the Jews who are in all the king's provinces." **8** "You may write in the king's name whatever pleases you concerning the Jews, and seal it with the royal signet ring. A document written in the king's name and sealed with the royal signet ring cannot be revoked." **11** The king's edict gave the Jews in each and every city the right to assemble and defend themselves, to destroy, kill, and annihilate every ethnic and provincial army hostile to them, including women and children, and to take their possessions as spoils of war. **15** Mordecai went from the king's presence clothed in royal purple and white, with a great gold crown and a purple robe of fine linen. The city of Susa shouted and rejoiced, **16** and the Jews celebrated with gladness, joy, and honor. **17** In every province and every city, wherever the king's command and his law reached, joy and rejoicing took place among the Jews. There was a celebration and a holiday. And many of the ethnic groups of the land professed themselves to be Jews because fear of the Jews had overcome them.

**9:1** The king's command and law went into effect on the thirteenth day of the twelfth month, the month Adar. On the day when the Jews' enemies had hoped to overpower them, just the opposite happened. The Jews overpowered those who hated them. **20** Mordecai recorded these events and sent letters to all the Jews in all of King Ahasuerus's provinces, both near and far. **21** He ordered them to celebrate the fourteenth and fifteenth days of the month Adar every year **22** because during those days the Jews got rid of their enemies. That was the month when their sorrow was turned into rejoicing and their mourning into a holiday. They were to be days of feasting, rejoicing, and of sending gifts to one another and the poor. **23** So the Jews agreed to continue the practice they had begun, as Mordecai had written them to do.

**10:3** Mordecai the Jew was second only to King Ahasuerus, famous among the Jews, and highly popular with many of his relatives. He continued to seek good for his people and to speak for the welfare of all his descendants.

have
ht, that
e unto
my fath
nay bu
the

58 EXPLORE THE BIBLE

# ❯ EXPLORE THE TEXT

## DEFENSE FOR GOD'S COVENANT PEOPLE
### (Esther 8:3-5,8,11)

Queen Esther was still feeling the weight of her guardian Mordecai's words to her: "Who knows, perhaps you have come to your royal position for such a time as this" (4:14). The king had made his favor and approval known to Esther on several occasions, yet as an irrevocable law of the Medes and Persians, the law to destroy the Jews remained in effect. Esther must still act faithfully.

Esther's consistently humble, temperate, and earnest character is again revealed as she pleaded with her husband, King Ahasuerus, "to revoke the evil of Haman the Agagite" (8:3; also see v. 5). Even though Esther was confident she could depend on her husband's favor and approval and Ahasuerus was steadfast in his extending the gold scepter toward his wife (see v. 4), they were both keenly aware that the established and published edict was irrevocable.

The words of the prophet Jeremiah may have been whispering in the minds of Esther and Mordecai, as well as any other Jew in the empire who was following "in the footsteps of the faith our father Abraham had" (Rom. 4:12). The invisible God had heralded through Jeremiah a couple of generations before, "Behold, I am the LORD, the God of all flesh. Is anything too hard for me?" (Jer. 32:27, ESV).

*What have you experienced that seemed to be impossible and could only be explained as God's work?*

Recognizing that the edict to destroy the Jews couldn't be revoked, Ahasuerus authorized Mordecai and Esther to "write in the king's name whatever pleases you concerning the Jews, and seal it with the royal signet ring" (Esth. 8:8). This law, too, couldn't be revoked. What, then, was this new law to be?

The new edict would grant the targeted covenant people, the Jews, "the right to assemble and defend themselves, to destroy, kill, and annihilate every ethnic and provincial army hostile to them, including women and children, and to take their possessions as spoils of war" (v. 11). Just as Haman had commanded the exact wording of the original edict, "written for each province in its own script and to each ethnic group in its own language" throughout the Persian Empire (3:12), so with this new edict, "everything was written exactly as Mordecai ordered for the Jews" and distributed to each of Persia's 127 provinces, "written for each province in its own script, for each ethnic group in its own language, and to the Jews in their own script and language" (8:9). The parallel language of the two edicts as recorded by the writer of Esther is obviously no more a coincidence than any of the other events recorded in this tapestry of the invisible God's providence.

## GOOD NEWS FOR GOD'S COVENANT PEOPLE
### (Esther 8:15-17)

The sin of pride was the source that gave rise to the first edict—a law of death. When the commandment came, "the city of Susa was in confusion," and "there was a great mourning among the Jewish people in every province where the king's command and edict came. They fasted, wept, and lamented, and many lay on sackcloth and ashes" (3:15; 4:3). The inescapable edict of condemnation rested on the head of each of God's covenant people. When the enemy of God's people was put to death and the good news of a defense against the law's death sentence was provided:

*The city of Susa shouted and rejoiced, and the Jews celebrated with gladness, joy, and honor. In every province and every city, wherever the king's command and his law reached, joy and rejoicing took place among the Jews. There was a celebration and a holiday.* **Esther 8:15-17**

Again, the parallel language is no coincidence. The king's edict bearing news of the preservation of life would reach as far as his edict bearing the former curse of death.

*How would you explain the bad news and good news of our salvation through the work of Jesus?*

The irony of God's providence is equally stunning. King Ahasuerus heeded Haman's counsel in an attempt to preserve the stability of his own empire for the posterity of his own people. Haman's evil scheme attempted to preserve his own life and fame. Both enterprises were proposed at the expense of the people of God. As providence would have it, however, the people of God were not only preserved but also exalted, while the "kingdoms" of both Ahasuerus and Haman eventually came to an end.

So hopeful was the news for the Jews yet so alarming for other peoples in the land that many of them "professed themselves to be Jews" (8:17) in hopes of avoiding the impending judgment. What was intended for evil as "the fate of all the Jews" (4:13) had been turned to good by their God and Savior (see Gen. 50:20).

*Into what temporary "kingdoms" are you tempted to put your hope?*

*How will you instead find your hope in the kingdom of God?*

# A HOLIDAY FOR GOD'S COVENANT PEOPLE
## (Esther 9:1,20-23; 10:3)

The events detailing Esther's ascension as the queen of the Persian Empire, as well as all God's provident works to rescue His covenant people, occurred as an example and were recorded for the instruction of all those who, like Esther, would follow Abraham's example of faith in the invisible God (see Rom. 4:12). The Book of Esther provides encouragement to trust that God remains Lord of all, even when circumstances might tempt us to doubt that. Surely no mere coincidence can explain Haman's demise, followed by that of his 10 sons on the very day determined by Haman's own casting of Pur (see Esth. 3:7; 9:10,14), even the very day "the king's command and law went into effect" (9:1).

The Book of Esther was also written to call all Jews to celebrate the festival of Purim. Mordecai, second in command only to King Ahasuerus of Persia, initiated this tradition when he ordered Jews throughout the empire "to celebrate the fourteenth and fifteenth days of the month Adar every year" (v. 21) to commemorate the surprise fate of all the Jews in which "their sorrow was turned into rejoicing and their mourning into a holiday" (v. 22; also see Ps. 30:11). The holiday was instituted "so that these days of Purim will not lose their significance in Jewish life and their memory will not fade from their descendants" (Esth. 9:28; also see vv. 29-32). The writer's mention of the date set for the fate of the Jews (no less than nine times: 3:7,13; 8:12; 9:1,15,17,18-21) attests to this purpose—a purpose that has evidently borne fruit, for Purim is celebrated to this day by Jews around the world.

Like Israel's Passover feast, all the festivals of God's Old Testament covenant people find their fulfillment in God's Son, Jesus Christ (see 2 Cor. 1:20). The commemoration of Purim, then, may be celebrated by all "who are of Abraham's faith" (Rom 4:16), "not with old yeast or with the yeast of malice and evil but with the unleavened bread of sincerity and truth" (1 Cor. 5:8). All who "belong to Christ [and therefore] are Abraham's seed, heirs according to the promise" (Gal. 3:29)—that is, Christians—celebrate Purim with a grander view of God's deliverance of His covenant people from the curse of death into the blessing of life by Jesus Christ. This salvation is the ultimate rescue from the fate of death by the invisible God, who providentially "works all things according to the counsel of his will" (Eph. 1.11, ESV).

## CONTINUED GOOD FOR GOD'S COVENANT PEOPLE *(Esther 10:3)*

The Book of Esther dispels the illusion of self-sufficiency. That is, neither the ingenuity, beauty, nor political authority of Esther or Mordecai could have provided salvation for their own lives or the lives of their people. The God who ordained their "sitting down, [their] going out and [their] coming in" (Isa. 37:28) and even the steps of the king is the only One who could preserve their security, whatever enemy threatened them.

A peasant girl named Hadassah, Esther, became the queen of the world. "Mordecai the Jew was second only to King Ahasuerus" (Esth. 10:3), the ruler of nearly half the world's population. In a Gentile empire Mordecai the Jew "continued to seek good for his people and to speak for the welfare of all his descendants" (v. 3). Only the invisible God, who providentially "brings down one and exalts another" (Ps. 75:7) and values His covenant people as "the apple of His eye" (Zech. 2:8, NASB), can ensure this kind of security and blessing for any people of faith, enabling them to appear as lights "in the midst of a crooked and perverse generation" (Phil. 2:15, NASB). Their hope for salvation from death is found in God alone.

**BIBLE SKILL**
**Compare Old and New Testament examples.**

*What do the following descriptions reveal about the importance of mourning and celebration through commemorative meals?*

*Exodus 12:14-28*

*Luke 22:14-20*

*How does each of these pictures of salvation ultimately point to Jesus?*

# ❯ OBEY THE TEXT

God's people share in the joy of salvation through Christ's intercession on our behalf. We did nothing to earn or deserve it. It is by His grace through faith we have been saved.

*Write your story—the story of how God saved you through Jesus and what has changed in your life now and forever as a result.*

*Identify specific people in your life who may not have experienced the life-changing, fate-reversing salvation of Jesus. Commit to share your story with them.*

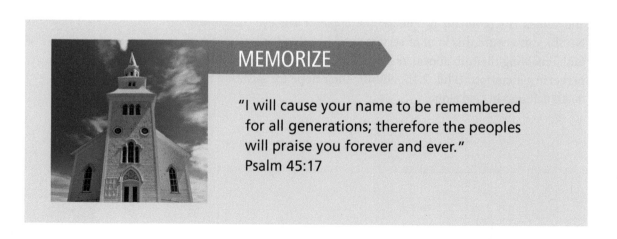

## MEMORIZE

"I will cause your name to be remembered for all generations; therefore the peoples will praise you forever and ever."
Psalm 45:17

Use the space provided to make observations and record prayer requests during the group experience for this session.

## MY THOUGHTS
Record insights and questions from the group experience.

_____

_____

_____

_____

_____

_____

## MY RESPONSE
Note specific ways you will put into practice the truth explored this week.

_____

_____

_____

_____

_____

_____

## MY PRAYERS
List specific prayer needs and answers to remember this week.

_____

_____

_____

_____

_____

_____

## ❯ GETTING STARTED

OPENING OPTIONS: **Choose one of the following to open the group discussion.**

WEEKLY QUOTATION DISCUSSION STARTER: "A godly woman's true adornment can't be bought at a department store or acquired in the beauty shop."—Dr. Tony Evans

> ❯ What's your initial response to this week's quotation?

> ❯ How do standards for physical beauty vary across cultures or throughout history?

> ❯ What qualities (physical and personality) are valued as attractive in men and women today?

The story of Esther begins in an environment where physical beauty was highly valued, but we'll see how inner character ultimately shaped the lives of the individuals and affected their community.

CREATIVE ACTIVITY: When the group has gathered, begin with a simple game. You'll say the first word listed below, along with the correct definition provided and two definitions that you make up. Group members will come to a consensus before guessing which is the correct definition. (Tip: the more bizarre but believable the options, the more engaging the game will be.) Then follow the same process with the other two words listed.

Philtrum: the groove between the upper lip and nose
Fulcrum: the point at which a lever pivots
Ferrule: the metal band joining pencil and eraser

Use the following questions to open the discussion.

> ❯ How did you decide what the answer was?

> ❯ Today we'll introduce a major theme and a common element in the Book of Esther—authority and advice. From whom do you ask advice? Why? To what do you look as an authority? Why?

## ❯ UNDERSTAND THE CONTEXT

PROVIDE BACKGROUND: Briefly introduce members to the Book of Esther by pointing out the major themes and any information or ideas that will help them understand Esther 1:10–2:20. Then, to help people personally connect today's context with the original context, ask the following questions.

> ❯ We'll see ironic contrasts throughout the Book of Esther. One major theme highlighted through irony is that of authority; people want power, but ultimately, God is sovereign and in control. Historically, how do men or women gain and maintain power?

> ❯ Why is it important to keep in mind that all events are ultimately within God's authority?

## ❯ EXPLORE THE TEXT

**READ THE BIBLE:** Ask a volunteer to read aloud Esther 1:10-12,15; 2:2,4-11,17,20.

**DISCUSS:** Use the following questions to discuss group members' initial reactions to the text.

> What was the underlying issue in the conflict that opens the Book of Esther?

> What do these verses reveal about the king? About the culture?

> Based on the details provided, what do you know about Mordecai? How would you contrast Mordecai's character with that of the king?

> Why is it significant that Esther is described as always following Mordecai's instruction? How does this detail emphasize an important contrast between Esther and Vashti, who are otherwise both described as exceedingly beautiful physically?

> What seemingly unfortunate or nonspiritual factors was God using to put people into positions of influence for reasons still unknown to those involved? What does God's activity in these areas reveal about His relationship to our daily lives—even the mundane details?

**NOTE:** Provide ample time for group members to share responses and questions about the text. Don't feel pressured to prioritize the printed agenda over group members' personal experiences. If time allows, discuss responses to the questions in the personal reading.

## ❯ OBEY THE TEXT

**RESPOND:** Foster an environment of openness and action. Help individuals apply biblical truth to specific areas of personal thought, attitude, and/or behavior.

> People who respond to advice or requests drive the action in the story of Esther. Where do you typically turn for advice about important decisions?

> When has bad advice or a proud reaction affected your life? How have your words or actions affected others?

> When has God used humility and seemingly fortunate circumstances to put you into a position of influence or into a significant relationship?

**PRAY:** Close by asking God to give you humility and wisdom in the middle of your circumstances, trusting that He's at work for a great purpose. Ask His Spirit to open your hearts and minds to what God wants to say to you during this study of the Book of Esther.

> ### GETTING STARTED

OPENING OPTIONS: **Choose one of the following to open the group discussion.**

WEEKLY QUOTATION DISCUSSION STARTER: "When you step out your door each day, do heaven, earth, and hell take notice?"—Dr. Tony Evans

> › What's your initial response to this week's quotation?

> › Today we'll look at maintaining integrity in the face of conflict. How can doing the right thing benefit you? How can it make you a target or seem to make life harder?

CREATIVE ACTIVITY: Before the group arrives, select at least four random things for which you instruct people to shout out the first ideas that pop into their heads as opposites. You may present print or electronic images, physical objects, or words, depending on your group. (Tip: the more random the object, the more fun the opposites will be.) After the game use the following questions to open the group discussion.

> › How are opposites helpful in describing and understanding things?

> › The Book of Esther constantly contrasts characters and circumstances to emphasize notable points. What would be the opposite of your favorite hobby? Your job? Your personality?

> ### UNDERSTAND THE CONTEXT

PROVIDE BACKGROUND: Briefly introduce group members to any information or ideas that will help them understand Esther 2:21–3:15. Then, to help them personally connect today's context with the original context, ask the following questions.

> › How could the emancipation of former slaves be strategic in encouraging conformity, submission, and unity among a kingdom?

> › Mordecai had instructed Esther not to volunteer information about her ethnicity. Why is it significant that the Jewish people were a minority group among a different culture?

> › When have you felt that it may be in your best interest to keep something about your beliefs, background, or family a secret?

## ❯ EXPLORE THE TEXT

**READ THE BIBLE:** Ask a volunteer to read aloud Esther 2:21-3:11,15.

**DISCUSS:** Use the following questions to discuss group members' initial reactions to the text.

> How would you describe Mordecai? How do the events described in these verses add to your understanding of his character?

> How would you describe Haman? How does he contrast with Mordecai?

> In your own words, explain the two conflicts presented in these verses and the two outcomes.

> How did Haman's anger extend beyond Mordecai's offense?

> What Christlike example and similarity are presented in these verses?

> What examples of God's providence are present in these verses?

**NOTE:** Provide ample time for group members to share responses and questions about the text. Don't feel pressured to prioritize the printed agenda over group members' personal experiences. If time allows, discuss responses to the questions in the personal reading.


## ❯ OBEY THE TEXT

**RESPOND:** Foster an environment of openness and action. Help individuals apply biblical truth to specific areas of personal thought, attitude, and/or behavior.

> When has standing on your conviction drawn negative attention or even caused hardship?

> What have you been made aware of that you needed to make known to someone else?

> Where do you need to take a stand, trusting and honoring God, even if it causes conflict?

> In what ways do you need to confess being like Haman, projecting your negative feelings onto a group of people? How will you repent of those feelings or actions?

**PRAY:** Close by praying for conviction of sin and confidence to live with integrity in the face of adversity and conflict. Ask for patience and humility in seeking God's approval, even if no earthly reward seems evident.

## ❯ GETTING STARTED

**OPENING OPTIONS: Choose one of the following to open the group discussion.**

**WEEKLY QUOTATION DISCUSSION STARTER:** "Give sorrow words. The grief that does not speak whispers the o'erfraught heart and bids it break."—William Shakespeare

> ❯ What's your initial response to this week's quotation?

> ❯ With good intentions people sometimes rush others to feel better when they actually need a healthy grieving process to feel and express sorrow. When have you experienced a healthy grieving process in which you deeply and honestly expressed sorrow? What gave you comfort?

**CREATIVE ACTIVITY:** Before the group arrives, select a negative news story that has dominated the headlines. Ask group members whether they're familiar with the story. Then use the following questions to open the group discussion.

> ❯ What other major news stories have been related to tragedy or fear?

> ❯ Why does bad news spread so quickly?

> ❯ What's the worst news you've ever had to share or hear?

> ❯ Today we're going to look at the ways Mordecai and Esther responded to bad news.

## ❯ UNDERSTAND THE CONTEXT

**PROVIDE BACKGROUND:** Briefly introduce group members to any information or ideas that will help them understand Esther 4:1-17. Then, to help them personally connect today's context with the original context, ask the following questions.

> ❯ Why might a king wish to distance himself from the emotions of his subjects, especially sadness?

> ❯ What are attitudes in our culture toward expressing or witnessing strong emotions, especially sadness? Are people generally comfortable or uncomfortable with expressions of emotion?

## ❯ EXPLORE THE TEXT

**READ THE BIBLE:** Ask a volunteer to read aloud Esther 4:1-4,8-17.

**DISCUSS:** Use the following questions to discuss group members' initial reactions to the text.

› Even in his sorrow and desperation, how did Mordecai demonstrate integrity?

› How would you summarize the interaction between Mordecai and Esther?

› How did the king's behavior toward the previous queen legitimize Esther's concern?

› What sobering warning did Mordecai offer in verse 13? How does this specific warning relate as a general principle to all God's people in regard to suffering?

› What evidence of faith in God's sovereignty and goodness is articulated in verse 14?

› How did Esther's response in verse 16 reveal faith in and relationship with God?

› How do these verses reveal the significance of God's people as a community?

› What does this conversation reveal about the source of hope for salvation and deliverance?

**NOTE:** Provide ample time for group members to share responses and questions about the text. Don't feel pressured to prioritize the printed agenda over group members' personal experiences. If time allows, discuss responses to the questions in the personal reading.


## ❯ OBEY THE TEXT

**RESPOND:** Foster an environment of openness and action. Help individuals apply biblical truth to specific areas of personal thought, attitude, and/or behavior.

› When was the last time you were deeply burdened for other people in your community?

› For what were you burdened, or for what are you burdened now?

› How will you respond?

› How can we pray and fast with you for this need?

› How can you encourage others to take action within their spheres of influence this week?

**PRAY:** Close with a time of prayer for one another. Share your burdens in confidence. Express any sorrows. Consider a time of fasting this week to focus on praying for the courage to respond to desperate situations or on behalf of those who are in need.

## > GETTING STARTED

**OPENING OPTIONS: Choose one of the following to open the group discussion.**

**WEEKLY QUOTATION DISCUSSION STARTER:** "Behind every specific call, whether it is to teach or preach or write or encourage or comfort, there is a deeper call that gives shape to the first: the call to give ourselves away—the call to die."—Michael Card

> What's your initial response to this week's quotation?

> What does it mean to give ourselves away, practically? What is the call to die as Christians?

**CREATIVE ACTIVITY:** Before the group arrives, identify several superheroes. When the group gathers, present print or electronic images, physical objects, or names of superheroes to play the game "Who would you rather be?" Using random pairs of superheroes, ask: "Who would you rather be— _____ or _____? Why?" After a few rounds, use the following questions to open the group discussion.

> Why do so many people love hero stories?

> Who was your childhood hero? Who is your current hero?

> In this session we'll contrast truly heroic and diabolical actions.

## > UNDERSTAND THE CONTEXT

**PROVIDE BACKGROUND:** Briefly introduce group members to any information or ideas that will help them understand Esther 5:1-14. Then, to help them personally connect today's context with the original context, ask the following questions.

> How were God's people in need of a literal savior to intercede on their behalf?

> How might Esther have felt, knowing that her culture didn't allow her to voluntarily approach the king?

> Do you feel that Esther's identity as a Jew made approaching the king easier or more difficult?

> What are modern examples of people who literally put their own lives at risk for the sake of others?

## ❯ EXPLORE THE TEXT

**READ THE BIBLE:** Ask a volunteer to read aloud Esther 5:1-10,14.

**DISCUSS:** Use the following questions to discuss group members' initial reactions to the text.

> Remembering that Esther had requested prayer and fasting from Mordecai and her maids for three days, what does verse 1 reveal about her actions? How might this simple detail point to faith in God's power?

> What answer to prayer immediately began relieving tension in verse 2?

> Knowing the urgent need motivating Esther to approach the king, how does her request demonstrate not only patience but also great faith and wisdom? How is it surprising?

> How do Haman's mood swings demonstrate the source of his security and personal worth?

> How would you contrast Esther's motives and conversation with those of Zeresh, the wife of Haman?

> How do these verses illustrate living selfishly or living selflessly?

**NOTE:** Provide ample time for group members to share responses and questions about the text. Don't feel pressured to prioritize the printed agenda over group members' personal experiences. If time allows, discuss responses to the questions in the personal reading.


## ❯ OBEY THE TEXT

**RESPOND:** Foster an environment of openness and action. Help individuals apply biblical truth to specific areas of personal thought, attitude, and/or behavior.

> Honestly, are the plans you make for the benefit of others, at your own risk, like Esther and Mordecai's plan? Or are your plans for your own benefit, even at the expense of others, like Haman's plan?

> Who in your community (or within your sphere of influence) needs an advocate to speak up and take action on their behalf—who may be helpless unless someone intercedes?

> How can you use your position, relationships, and influence for God's work to save others?

> What will you do to humble yourself and trust God this week?

**PRAY:** Close by asking someone to lead the group in prayer. Encourage this member to pray for everyone to seek ways to join God's work this week.

## ❯ GETTING STARTED

**OPENING OPTIONS: Choose one of the following to open the group discussion.**

**WEEKLY QUOTATION DISCUSSION STARTER:** "Even when things seem to be going wrong, they just could be going right because when you're in God's will, the negatives are part of his positive program."—Dr. Tony Evans

> ❯ What's your initial response to this week's quotation?

> ❯ What are some specific examples in the Bible of God's working for His greater good through a situation that looked bad? In history? In your life?

**CREATIVE ACTIVITY:** Before the group arrives, select an object to drop on the floor as an illustration. (Tip: an object that makes a loud noise will be more dramatic.) When the group gathers, begin by standing and dropping the object for everyone to witness. You may want to ask everyone to participate. Then use the following questions to open the group discussion.

> ❯ What will always happen when we hold this object up and let it go? Why?

> ❯ How do you know gravity is real if you can't see it?

> ❯ In this session we'll begin to see more clearly the effects of the invisible hand of God at work.

## ❯ UNDERSTAND THE CONTEXT

**PROVIDE BACKGROUND:** Briefly introduce group members to any information or ideas that will help them understand Esther 6:1–8:2. Then, to help them personally connect today's context with the original context, ask the following questions.

> ❯ Esther is the only book of the Bible in which the name of God never appears; nevertheless, God was sovereign over seemingly fortunate, ironic, and coincidental circumstances throughout the story. In what circumstance is God seemingly invisible in the world today, but you trust that He's working behind the scenes without being acknowledged?

> ❯ In what areas of life do you feel anxiety or tension, wondering how God will possibly work things out for good?

## ❯ EXPLORE THE TEXT

**READ THE BIBLE:** Ask a volunteer to read aloud Esther 6:1-3,6-11; 7:1-6,10; 8:1-2.

**DISCUSS:** Use the following questions to discuss group members' initial reactions to the text.

> What evidence do you see of God's ability to work in the lives of people who don't know or acknowledge Him—specifically the king?

> How did the delayed reward for Mordecai's previous actions prove to be perfect timing, not just for his sake but for the greater community?

> In what other ways is God's sovereignty evident in this story? His justice? His salvation?

> What great reversals took place in the lives of Mordecai and Haman?

> How do the plans of people contrast with the providence of God?

> How did Esther continue to seek the welfare of others rather than just personal benefit?

**NOTE:** Provide ample time for group members to share responses and questions about the text. Don't feel pressured to prioritize the printed agenda over group members' personal experiences. If time allows, discuss responses to the questions in the personal reading.

## ❯ OBEY THE TEXT

**RESPOND:** Foster an environment of openness and action. Help individuals apply biblical truth to specific areas of personal thought, attitude, and/or behavior.

> How does the invisible hand of God, which was at work in the story of Esther, encourage you in your life today?

> When have you delayed obedience or steps of faith, unsure about how things would work out?

> What will you do to trust God's perfect timing this week—both His justice and His blessing?

**PRAY:** Close by thanking God for His power, His timing, His justice, and His blessings—most significantly, our salvation through Jesus Christ. Reflect on the fact that Jesus' life, death, and resurrection were the ultimate acts of sovereign power, justice, mercy, blessing, and salvation, reversing the fate of our Enemy and of all God's people in His perfect timing.

## ❭ GETTING STARTED

**OPENING OPTIONS: Choose one of the following to open the group discussion.**

**WEEKLY QUOTATION DISCUSSION STARTER:** "Legacy is much more than simply passing on the family name. Legacy involves passing on a kingdom worldview and perspective."—Dr. Tony Evans

> ❭ What's your initial response to this week's quotation?

> ❭ Who has most influenced your view of life and God's kingdom?

> ❭ How would you like to be remembered?

**CREATIVE ACTIVITY:** Before the group arrives, prepare treats and beverages. (Tip: if a potluck meal or an assortment of desserts can be planned in advance with group members, that's ideal.) After everyone has food and a beverage, use the following questions to open the group discussion.

> ❭ How does sharing food and beverages change the mood of a gathering?

> ❭ Why do people often celebrate with food and beverages?

> ❭ What's your favorite holiday or tradition? Why?

> ❭ In this final session we'll see how a story that has revolved around eating and drinking, feasting and fasting, concludes with a new celebration.

## ❭ UNDERSTAND THE CONTEXT

**PROVIDE BACKGROUND:** Briefly introduce group members to any information or ideas that will help them understand Esther 8:3–10:3. Then, to help them personally connect today's context with the original context, ask the following questions.

> ❭ The Book of Esther ends with an explanation of why it was recorded: to commemorate the salvation of the Jewish people and the establishment of the Feast of Purim, a celebration still observed in modern-day Jewish tradition. Why is it important for a community to remember important moments in its history?

> ❭ What's the benefit of celebrating as an individual? As a community? As a church or small group?

## ❯ EXPLORE THE TEXT

**READ THE BIBLE:** Ask a volunteer to read aloud Esther 8:3-5,8,11,15-17; 9:1,20-23; 10:3.

**DISCUSS:** Use the following questions to discuss group members' initial reactions to the text.

> In what way do these verses (and the Book of Esther as a whole) reveal a culture that respected the authority of the written law and the power of a name and someone's word?

> How did the reversal of fates that began with Haman and Mordecai extend to the people throughout the kingdom? How did God not only save but also bless His people?

> Why were Jews throughout the kingdom told to celebrate? Why is it significant that the customs of Purim were observed annually throughout the generations?

> What legacy did Mordecai leave?

> What would you say is the major theme(s) of Esther? Why is this book part of Scripture, even though it never explicitly mentions God, His laws, or His worship?

> What's the most significant insight you'll take away from this study of Esther?

**NOTE:** Provide ample time for group members to share responses and questions about the text. Don't feel pressured to prioritize the printed agenda over group members' personal experiences. If time allows, discuss responses to the questions in the personal reading.

## ❯ OBEY THE TEXT

**RESPOND:** Foster an environment of openness and action. Help individuals apply biblical truth to specific areas of personal thought, attitude, and/or behavior.

> Name at least one person to whom you can you pass on the good news of God's work.

> What will you do to be sure they know what God has done to save them?

> How will you invite them to join the celebration as part of God's covenant people?

> How will you intentionally celebrate and express the joy of your salvation this week?

**PRAY:** Close with a prayer of commitment to be intentional about sharing the knowledge of God and the joy of salvation through Jesus.

# ❯TIPS FOR LEADING A GROUP

## PRAYERFULLY PREPARE

Prepare for each session by—

> ❯ **reviewing the weekly material and group questions ahead of time;**
> ❯ **praying for each person in the group.**

Ask the Holy Spirit to work through you and the group discussion to help people take steps toward Jesus each week as directed by God's Word.

## MINIMIZE DISTRACTIONS

Create a comfortable environment. If group members are uncomfortable, they'll be distracted and therefore not engaged in the group experience. Plan ahead by taking into consideration—

> ❯ **seating;**
> ❯ **temperature;**
> ❯ **lighting;**
> ❯ **food or drink;**
> ❯ **surrounding noise;**
> ❯ **general cleanliness (put pets away if meeting in a home).**

At best, thoughtfulness and hospitality show guests and group members they're welcome and valued in whatever environment you choose to gather. At worst, people may never notice your effort, but they're also not distracted. Do everything in your ability to help people focus on what's most important: connecting with God, with the Bible, and with others.

## INCLUDE OTHERS

**Your goal is to foster a community in which people are welcome just as they are but encouraged to grow spiritually.** Always be aware of opportunities to—

> ❯ **invite** new people to join your group;
> ❯ **include** any people who visit the group.

An inexpensive way to make first-time guests feel welcome or to invite people to get involved is to give them their own copies of this Bible study book.

## ENCOURAGE DISCUSSION

A good small group has the following characteristics.

> **Everyone participates.** Encourage everyone to ask questions, share responses, or read aloud.

> **No one dominates—not even the leader.** Be sure what you say takes up less than half of your time together as a group. Politely redirect discussion if anyone dominates.

> **Nobody is rushed through questions.** Don't feel that a moment of silence is a bad thing. People often need time to think about their responses to questions they've just heard or to gain courage to share what God is stirring in their hearts.

> **Input is affirmed and followed up.** Make sure you point out something true or helpful in a response. Don't just move on. Build personal connections with follow-up questions, asking how other people have experienced similar things or how a truth has shaped their understanding of God and the Scripture you're studying. People are less likely to speak up if they fear that you don't actually want to hear their answers or that you're looking for only a certain answer.

> **God and His Word are central.** Opinions and experiences can be helpful, but God has given us the truth. Trust Scripture to be the authority and God's Spirit to work in people's lives. You can't change anyone, but God can. Continually point people to the Word and to active steps of faith.

## KEEP CONNECTING

Think of ways to connect with group members during the week. Participation during the group session is always improved when members spend time connecting with one another away from the session. The more people are comfortable with and involved in one another's lives, the more they'll look forward to being together. When people move beyond being friendly and in the same group to truly being friends who form a community, they come to each session eager to engage instead of merely attending.

Encourage group members with thoughts, commitments, or questions from the session by connecting through—

> emails;
> texts;
> social media.

When possible, build deeper friendships by planning or spontaneously inviting group members to join you outside your regularly scheduled group time for—

> meals;
> fun activities;
> projects around your home, church, or community.

# ❯ GROUP CONTACT INFORMATION

Name _____ Number _____
Email _____

Name _____ Number _____
Email _____

Name _____ Number _____
Email _____

Name _____ Number _____
Email _____

Name _____ Number _____
Email _____

Name _____ Number _____
Email _____

Name _____ Number _____
Email _____

Name _____ Number _____
Email _____

Name _____ Number _____
Email _____

Name _____ Number _____
Email _____

Name _____ Number _____
Email _____